HOW TO MARRY A FINNISH GIRL

PHIL SCHWARZMANN

HOW TO MARRY A FINNISH GIRL

EVERYTHING YOU WANT TO KNOW ABOUT FINLAND, THAT FINNS WON'T TELL YOU

GUMMERUS

© Phillip Schwarzmann and Gummerus Publishers 2011

Viides painos

Kustantaja:
Gummerus Kustannus Oy
Helsinki

Painopaikka:
Nørhaven
Tanska 2012

ISBN 978-951-20-9010-5

To Anja, my Finnish girl –
the only woman I've ever loved,
and ever will love.

ABOUT THE AUTHOR

Phil Schwarzmann has lived in Finland for...too long. He came to Finland for love, and ten years later he's still in love. He works for a large Finnish mobile phone manufacturer that shall remain nameless. His Finnish is terrible because he graduated from American public schools. In his free time he performs stand-up comedy and blogs about Finland. His dog has his own Facebook page. He lives in Helsinki with his Finnish girlfriend. He wrote a book about marriage but is not, and never was, married. He has a love-hate relationship with Finland—it's complicated. It has something to do with the winters.

Don't take anything he says or writes too seriously.

Read more about Phil from www.philschwarzmann.com or follow him on Twitter @philschwarzmann.

TABLE OF CONTENTS

INTRODUCTION

BRAVO!

Congratulations on your purchase of *How to Marry a Finnish Girl*! Or maybe I should say "Congratulations on borrowing this book from a friend!" Or maybe it's better to say "Congratulations on grudgingly accepting this book from a friend!" And now every time you see that friend, she will ask how you enjoyed the book. You promise to read it soon! You see that friend once more, she again asks how's the book – you respond the same. After a few more times, you HATE that friend, and avoid her whenever possible. Once a best friend, this person is now your archenemy – all thanks to this book.

THE 30-DAY GUARANTEE

This book guarantees that you will marry a Finnish girl in thirty days or less! She may not be the most beautiful girl in Finland, but she will be more attractive than anyone you could snag in your homeland. She will also be able to gut a fish quicker than anyone from your town. Can any other book offer you that? No.

"Thirty Days? That's fast!"

Yes, if you follow the instructions thoroughly, and laugh at all the cleverly-crafted jokes, you'll be at your wedding thirty days from now. In fact, by the end of this chapter, you will kiss your first Finnish girl. In twenty-four hours, you will enjoy a sauna with her. Naked. In seventy-two hours you will have moved into her 30sq/m apartment. In two weeks you both will have moped around the house for several days without talking. And after sixty days she will bear your first-born child. Guaranteed.

@philschwarzmann – The definition of a "good sense of humor" is someone who laughs at your bad jokes.

Everything You Want to Know About Finland That Finns Won't Tell You

Unlike any other book, *How to Marry a Finnish Girl* takes you through the REAL Finland experience—the experience Finns don't want you to know about.

By the end of chapter one, you will have purchased a one-way ticket to Finland and won the lottery. By the end of chapter two, you will have found an apartment and been featured on the front page of Finland's trashiest tabloid. By the end of chapter three you will have survived Juhannus and avoided serving in the Finnish army. By the end of chapter four you'll know which tastes better, McDonald's or Hesburger. By the end of chapter five you'll be fighting off Finnish women with a stick. By the end of chapter six you'll get paid to surf Facebook all day. By the end of chapter seven you'll not only be speaking Finnish, you'll be teaching it. And by the end of chapter eight you'll be on holiday at Finland's Disneyworld.

DON'T LET FINNS READ THIS BOOK!!

When a Finn asks, "How do you like Finland?" there is but one answer, and one answer only.... "I LOVE IT!" Feel free to use expletives. "I FUCKING LOVE IT!" Finns find English curse words acceptable and humorous.

Finns love to hear foreigners' thoughts on their country, but only the good things. After decades of being painfully ignored by the world, Finland would rather remain ignored than be criticized. Foreigners are allowed to list all the great stereotypical aspects of Finland: The midnight sun, lush forests, clean air and water, safe cities, great skiing, great schools, a strong army, fantastic welfare benefits, the best hockey in the world, and of course, Finnish women.

While Finns complain about Finland all day long—foreigners are forbidden to join in. Foreigners may only joke about a few aspects of Finland: reindeer-piss beer, quiet Finns, high taxes, mämmi, drinking habits, the KKK-Market, long winters, Danny, and of course, Finnish women.

How to Marry a Finnish Girl respectfully ignores any unwritten rules and taboos placed upon foreigners. Those who were expecting yet another brouhaha book about Finland will be disappointed. Though this book is full of stereotypes, generalizations, over simplifications, cynicism, exaggerations, and outright lies—Finns are, above all, honest, self-depreciative, and have the best sense of humor in the world...they, and you, will hopefully enjoy these observations. And maybe laugh a little on the way.

But just to be safe, don't let Finns read this book. Please don't show it to members of Perussuomalaiset either.

@philschwarzmann – If you live in a country long enough
that you write a book about it…it's too long.

THE CAST OF CHARACTERS

Throughout *How to Marry a Finnish Girl* you'll come across a few reoccurring characters. Let's go through them.

You

You came to Finland for love. Or maybe Nokia. Or maybe both. Or maybe you love death metal, hockey, or F1. Maybe your family migrated to Minnesota or Australia and you have a calling to return to the motherland. Maybe you're taking advantage of free school in Finland. Maybe free unemployment checks.

You're in your twenties, kinda smart, kinda dumb, kinda tired of where you been living the past twenty years. You didn't choose Finland, Finland chose you. But you're here now and plan to make the most of it—a plane ticket home is not an option. You came to Finland as one person, and will leave as another. You may not have come to Finland for love, but it's the reason you stay.

Mari

Mari is what brought you to Finland. Mari is what keeps you in Finland. Mari is why you left Finland. Mari is not your typical Finnish woman. When you first met it was something out of a fairytale. She was the most beautiful thing you'd ever seen. Nothing has brought you more joy in your life—she's the best thing to ever happen to you.

Pekka

Pekka is your quintessential Finnish man. A man of many thoughts, but few words. Pekka loves you, that's why you moved here, but there's nothing he loves more than competitive sports, a gadget to fix, a beer in the sauna, and solitude alongside a lake.

STORY: My name is 'Phil', but all my neighborhood kids think it's 'Pili'. On my way to work each morning they say "rnol moi, Pili!" as they laugh. I can't believe I moved to the only country in the world where my name means 'penis'. We Phil's don't get any respect in Finland or elsewhere. In films, if a character named Phil is introduced halfway through the movie, he's about to get shot. We Phil's don't last very long in movies. It's never "Phil the Barbarian" or "Phil Claude Van Damme".

1 A ONE-WAY TICKET TO FINLAND

WELCOME TO HEAVEN ON EARTH

Congratulations. You met a cute Finnish girl on the internet. She's convinced you that Finland is heaven on earth and you should move there. Since you're not doing much with your life at the moment, and you're not going to get a girl of this caliber in your hometown, you figure "screw it", why not migrate?

Migrating to a foreign country brings a lot of questions to mind. "How will I make money?" "Will I learn the language?" "What will my parents think?" "What happens if this chick dumps me in a few months?" "How will I cope with the metric system?"

You decide to do a little research. First you learn that Finns love Finland. They're a patriotic bunch, possibly the most patriotic in the world. There are Finns still alive today who lived under Russian rule. Finland's independence is a recent memory for the entire country and Finland's Independence Day is much more than a hot dog and hamburger jubilee.

Finns are taught in school at an early age that Finland is the best country in the world. Its greatness isn't an opinion but rather a matter of fact. It's said that, "Being born in Finland is like winning the lottery." So very true, if you consider the "lottery" to be a 5€ scratch-off ticket.

Of course, like any country, there are great things and not-so-great things. (Unless you live in Norway where there are only great things.) So you make a list of all the great reasons to move to Finland. Then, if your Finnish girlfriend hasn't ripped the pages out already, a list of all the reasons why you should remain in Liverpool and keep calling that gap-toothed redhead you've been messing around with since middle school.

Top 10 Reasons Why You SHOULD Move to Finland

WOMEN: Sometimes it feels like this is the *only* reason to live in Finland, hence the #1 spot. It's such an important reason that an entire chapter is devoted to it in this book.

SAFETY: Finland is one of the safest countries in the world – until you, the foreigner, arrive and do what foreigners do best: crime. Helsinki certainly *looks* safer thanks to its whiteness – and that's all that really matters, isn't it?

NATURE: One of the most sparsely populated countries in Europe, Finland is like a giant wildlife nature preserve that you can legally live in. If you like moose more than humans, you've found your home.

LIBERALISM: Imagine a world where the left-wing rule! A world where both the prime minster and president were women. A world where "right-wingers" fight to get value-added taxes down to a puny twenty-three percent. A world where tax evasion is more serious than rape. In Finland, everyone is equal and equally miserable.

SIMPLICITY: Life gets so complicated, doesn't it? Keeping up with both the rat race and the Joneses is a race you'll never win. So why not give up and focus on what really matters: Family, hockey, your dog, shoveling snow at your townhouse in Espoo, your prized Toyota Avensis station wagon with the big rims, and putting together IKEA furniture.

WHITE PEOPLE: You know you love'em. Finland is full of them. "Finally, a country where everyone looks just like me! But even WHITER!"

WORK-LIFE BALANCE: Work can be such drag. Consider five weeks of holiday, or an unlimited amount of sick days, or leaving to pick up your children at 3:30pm, or retiring at age twenty-five due to depression.

ENGLISH: Finns speak excellent English. You could literally spend your entire life in Finland and never learn a word of Finnish. Many foreigners do, they're known as, "The British".

FREE SCHOOL: If your parents didn't save for your college tuition because daddy wanted a new SUV every two years, and mommy gave up on her career long ago to have you, then Finland is your ticket to education. Sure you could enlist in the military and get your face blown off by an Iraqi teenager, but why not get a free masters degree in Finland and get blown off by hot drunken Finnish girls.

WELFARE STATE: Free healthcare, free schooling, free daycare, free lunch and a free needle exchange. Of course, virtually everything else is insanely expensive. As they say, "The welfare state ain't well fair!"

@philschwarzmann – They say Finnish women
are like wine, they get better with age –
man I can't wait until my girlfriend is like 102!

Top 10 Reasons Why You Should Stay Home

WEATHER: Sometimes it seems this is the *only* reason to hate Finland, hence the #1 spot. Six months of solid cold weather and snow. Finns will keep telling you, "But you see...Finnish summers are so GREAT!" You know where else summer is great? EVERYWHERE. It's *summer*.

DARKNESS: If the weather doesn't kill you, the darkness will. It's impossible to wake up in the mornings, and you start getting sleepy at 3pm.

COSTS: Twenty-three percent value added tax and income tax that is up to sixty percent. Combine that with low wages, and you live in one of the world's most expensive countries. There's no such thing as a free lunch, not even for a Finnish girl on a date.

LACK OF DIVERSITY: Life in a country full of people that look identical to yourself is titillating for about a day. Soon you'll miss all that diversity brings: New cultures, new experiences, new opinions, a better gene pool, and most importantly—kebab.

LOCATION: Finland might as well be an island at the top of the earth, no one dares to drive to mainland Europe through Russia or, gasp, Sweden. You'll need an expensive plane ticket to get anywhere. Finns unknowingly joke that they're, "Going on holiday to Europe this summer," as if Finland isn't already part of Europe.

FOOD & DRINK: Ever heard of "Finnish food"? Neither have the Finns. Finland's meat & potato society isn't much for experimenting with new cuisine. Meanwhile, Finland's drink selection is limited to what the state-run "Alko" shops carry. But if you're into mild lagers, Finland has a dozen to choose from, each tasting identical.

HOUSING: An apartment in a city with a population of half a million should be cheap, right? Wrong. Finland's housing space is tiny, and Helsinki has some of the most expensive housing in the world. If you want cheap housing, move to Vantaa! LOL!

DIFFICULT LANGUAGE: Finnish is darn near impossible, especially for the well educated and gainfully employed foreigner. You won't learn it, so don't even bother.

UNEMPLOYMENT: Unemployment is high – finding a job in Finland is tough, especially for a foreigner who doesn't speak the world's hardest language. Fortunately, unemployment benefits are great.

WEATHER: This is worth mentioning this twice.

WHAT KIND OF PEOPLE MOVE TO FINLAND?

Finns always wonder why anyone would move here. Generally foreigners in Finland fall into one of the following groups below:

HORNY BOYS: This group seems to constitute about 99 percent of all immigrants to Finland. Some ugly, dorky guy meets a beautiful, intelligent Finnish girl—probably online—then travels half way around the world to be with her.

HORNY GIRLS: This is rare. Not too many women would migrate thousands of miles for a Finnish man. Estonians, Russians, and Asians are the exception.

@philschwarzmann – YLE: "Police Raid Helsinki Strip Clubs in Search for Illegal Foreign Workers" …and find lots of Poles.

WORKERS AND STUDENTS: School is free, and IT jobs are plentiful! A couple years in Finland couldn't be that bad, right? It's not Sweden but it's darn near close. This group only plans to stay here temporarily, but often gets sucked into permanent status (see "Horny Boys" above).

SOMALI REFUGEES, VIETNAMESE REFUGEES, AND SERBIAN REFUGEES: Every decade, Finland graciously allows in one ethnic group who are down on their luck. Finland isn't usually a refugee's first choice. Thanks to Finland's animosity towards foreigners and its cold weather, refugees shop around to other countries before they make the decision: Civil War back home or a tiny apartment in East Helsinki.

VILLE VALO CHASERS: Do you feel strongly that "glam metal" is awesome but "thrash metal" sucks? Then Finland is your Mecca, and you're very disturbed. One of Finland's largest exports is heavy metal, with the country producing dozens of international acts each year. Lead singer of the Finnish "love metal" band HIM, Ville Valo, is a sexual goddess amongst socially awkward girls with pale skin and dull tattoos. Fans of Ville and the genre make pilgrimages to the country each year, or at the very least, spend a lot of time on Finland's Wikipedia page.

ANCESTORS: Finns migrate away from Finland yet their children move back. During the nineteenth century many Finns immigrated to Canada and northern parts of the United States. A century later a fair number of Finns immigrated to Australia and New Zealand. Their offspring return to the motherland in search of their roots, with the half-baked Finnish they learned from home.

LONERS: So you're wanted by the mob, or maybe you got pregnant by a Japanese businessman and an abortion will dishonor your family. Do you just want to get away from everyone and everything? Did you close your eyes, spin a globe, and choose the furthest inhabited place up north? In Finland, no one looks you in the eyes or gets involved in your business. It's the perfect getaway!

WHY DO PEOPLE GET TRAPPED IN FINLAND FOREVER?

When moving to Finland there's a risk you'll fall in love and never want to leave. You might arrive and say, "I'm here just for a couple years!" Before you know it those couple years turn into a blonde wife, two kids, and a row house in Vantaa. Year after year you say, "This is the year I'm heading home!" But, after a time, the definition of "home" becomes blurred and though you can, at anytime, leave Finland, the outside world is scary. Plus your ex-wife is keeping the kids in Finland.

With this in mind, below is a list of reasons why foreigners get trapped in Finland along with tips on avoiding other foreigners' mistakes.

TRAP #1: "Life in Finland is So Easy!"

Life in Finland is almost like retiring early. Life's little annoyances all but disappear. No more traffic congestion, no more pressure to volunteer at the soup kitchen, no more pissed off McDonald's cashiers, and no more expensive electric bills from running your air-conditioner.

TIP: Finland has made you soft! Nothing worthwhile in life is easy. Make life difficult again: Develop a drinking problem. This will keep your friends and family on their toes at all times, especially during holidays and BBQs. As life in Finland is so mind-numbingly easy, you need to get knocked out by a bouncer in Kontula to remind you that you're still alive.

TRAP #2: "Finland is So Safe!"

Finland has the third highest number of firearms per capita in the world (1st is the United States, 2nd Yemen) yet they're rarely shot at humans, but rather harmless, innocent animals frolicking in the forest. You'll never hear about a "bad neighborhood" in Finland's cities—unless someone is talking about how lame Kallio is. So go ahead and put your kindergartener on the public bus, sleep soundly while your teenager parties it up at night, pass out on the train, or get hammered at noon on a Tuesday and harass the general public—no one will harm you. Finland is the safest place on the planet, even if statistics say otherwise.

TIP: Live in East Helsinki. It's the closest thing to having a hometown kind of feel.

TRAP #3: "My Wife Won't Leave Finland!"

And why would she? Remember, Finland is the BEST country on the planet. Better than East and West Germany COMBINED! So who'd want to throw away that winning lottery ticket? No matter where you're from: it's not as safe as Finland, not as easy as Finland, not as pretty as Finland, not as Finnish as Finland—and unless you're from Winnipeg, it's way too hot.

TIP: Convince her to move back to your homeland "just for a year". Make some babies then refuse to return to Finland—after all, the kids can never leave their current country unless both parents agree. But be warned, Finnish women are notorious for "kidnapping" their children back to Finland, and the entire Finnish nation supports this.

TRAP #4: "My Wife Divorced Me and I Have Kids!"

So your wife read tip #3 before you did. Life in Finland has become so "easy" that you're now overweight, a tad alcoholic, and quite dull. Mari is more interested in the kids than your Fantasy Football team—so she left. She's definitely not going to move abroad and give up the sweet free dentistry Finland offers. Nor will she give up her kids. And if you leave the country, you're a bastard father.

TIP: Don't have kids. Ever. Especially in a foreign country. And if she did "forget" to take the pill and you woke up one day with a couple of rugrats, go ahead and move abroad without them—in today's day and age, following your kid's Twitter account is good enough parenting.

TRAP #5: "I've Contracted Hot Blonde Syndrome!"

Finland's nationalist party once said, "foreigners steal Finnish women." But getting Finnish women is like stealing MP3s off the internet—it's easy. You can't get a woman like this in London, and as you read from trap #3, you won't lure one back with you. So you're stuck.

TIP: You may want to try other parts of Northern Europe for your hot blonde syndrome fix: Sweden, Denmark, Norway, Russia, Estonia, or Latvia are all excellent choices. You can even travel to Minnesota or Michigan to find Americans who are part Finnish—the only problem is, the other part is Sasquatch.

TRAP #6: "They Keep Paying Me!"

You've tried coming in late, you've tried disappearing for entire afternoons, you've tried racial slurs, sexual harassment, monitor theft, and entire days devoted to Facebook—but once you're on a Finnish company's payroll, it's impossible to get off. Xeroxing your butt will never be tolerated so lightly back in your home country.

TIP: Take the workplace harassment up a notch: Instead of making fun of Russians, make fun of Swedish-speaking Finns. At the water cooler, boast about the cooler's "big jugs" then refer to the tap as a "nipple". Steal an entire server. Setup a Twitter account for your penis and tell your co-workers that your penis is now "following you". You'll be on Finnish unemployment in no time, earning 80 percent of your original salary for years to come.

TRAP #7: "My Homeland is Even Worse!"

So you're from Haiti, Vietnam, Afghanistan, or South Africa (Johannesburg, not Cape Town). Finland truly is heaven on earth, as it's been several weeks since you've been shot at by children. You can't go back home, as "home" has been pillaged by rebel forces and is now governed by a band of wild dogs—and you realize your passport is nothing more than a fake treasure map from a Burger King kids meal.

TIP: Change your name to "Pekka", get Finnish citizenship, and move to the south coast of Spain.

HOW TO FIT-IN IN FINLAND?

Be white. Even people with a suntan are viewed suspiciously. Finns are a fine looking group of people. Some may argue they're the most beautiful people in the world. The men are handsome, the women even more so. Every woman is a serious Miss Finland contender, every man a possible Scandinavian Hunk.

Finns have a unique blend of Western and Eastern European looks, in particular, the Eastern European high cheekbones. Is there anything sexier? Maybe back dimples...

Anyhow, if high cheekbones are your thing, Finland is your dreamland.

There are essentially six kinds of finns:

THE ENGINEER: Finnish engineers have no idea what clothes to buy, so their wives do all the shopping. They wear whichever short-sleeved plaid shirt Mari bought from Dressmann. The color of the shirt need not matter, as long as it's made from a material that does not need ironing. Brown loafers are required, belts are not. Khaki pants must ride high on the waist. During the summer months it's brown sandals (with socks) and capri-pants riding high. The most popular haircut is "balding, with an inner-tube of hair around the head". The face should be clean-shaven, although most engineers cannot grow facial hair, and for those who can, it generally comes in patchy. Glasses must be at least fifteen-years old. Jewelry should consist of a wedding ring and meaningless gold chain around the neck.

THE BUSINESSMAN: See "Engineer" and add a wrinkled sports coat (dry cleaning is insanely expensive in Finland), black belt (yes, even with brown loafers), and trendy-but-not-so-trendy spectacles.

THE MIDDLE AGED MOMMY: She has short hair. After all she's been struggling with long hair all her life and now, sitting home everyday on maternity leave for the next few years , why bother looking attractive? And if you're in the male-dominated business world, the short hair makes you blend in more easily with your male colleagues. This Mommy wears, "trendy" eyeglasses that hide what, if any, good looks she has left. She gets bonus points if the color of her glasses match the color of her dyed hair. If this is your disguise, don't wear heels, it's a dead giveaway you're a foreigner. And don't have eyebrows, again, that's a dead giveaway that you're a foreigner.

THE COUNTRY BUMPKIN: Comfort is key here. The classiest place you'll visit during the week is the Chilean red wine section of Alko, so "dress to depress" as they say. Men—a twenty-year old tracksuit is appropriate cause at any moment you may have the urge to go cross-country skiing. Women—an aging Marimekko shirt, blue jeans, and old white sneakers. If you want to dye your hair, dye it some shade of red, orange, or purple. Men—if there's a situation where you need to dress up, like for instance, taking a trip to the next town over, wear a tie, just make sure it's the same one you wore in high school. Jewelry should consist of the Finnish Lion dangling from a cheap gold chain.

THE TEENAGER: Want to know what the current teenage fashion is? Visit Sweden, have a look around, then wait five years...that's what Finnish teens look like. Finnish girls have an arsenal of skin products. They'll apply these each night, and each morning she'll cover herself in a mask full of makeup to mimic a Barbie Doll. Look at a Finnish girl from the side and you can actually see where the mask begins and ends—there's not a millimeter exposed on her face, and they wonder why their skin is so bad.

THE CHILD: This one is simple—for boys, a blue jumpsuit. For girls, a red one. Finnish children are like penguins, it's impossible to tell them apart, they all wear the exact same jumpsuits year round. In fact it's surprising more Finnish parents don't accidentally take home the wrong child from daycare. And it doesn't matter if it's +15°C (59F) or −15°C (5F), all Finnish children must wear hats and gloves.

STORY: My Finnish girlfriend and I met on a Caribbean cruise in 2000. I discovered that she was an architect, and assumed she was wealthy. She was excited to meet an American, and assumed I was wealthy. Turns out architects in Finland are poor, and not all Americans have money. We were both very disappointed, and remain so still to this day.

2 FINLAND, THE FINNS, AND YOU

WHERE SHOULD I LIVE?

You probably won't have much of a choice. Mari already picked out a nice little apartment outside of the city back when she was with her former boyfriend. It's a quaint, quiet, and rather new-ish apartment on the second floor, over looking a playground and shopping center. You immediately feel right at home. You think you could live here forever—but that's only because Mari's house has just been a little love den for the two of you. When three times a day soon becomes three times a week, and you find her ex-boyfriend's Magnum-brand condoms under the bed, you're ready to move and get a fresh start.

@phIlschwarzmann – Finns don't chit-chat on elevators, cause Finnish elevators barely fit one person.

You're an unemployed bum. Should you live in that Finnish city by the lake with the S-market and K-market? Or how about that other Finnish city by the lake with the S-market and K-market? Finnish cities are all so very different!

So where should you move out? Answer: Helsinki.

Okay, granted, an abrupt answer like that doesn't make for an interesting chapter. Let's elaborate: Helsinki, but only the parts within Ring I.

Too specific for you? Let's expand that: Helsinki, but only the parts within Ring I, and only the parts that are a fifteen minute walk from Stockmann's—specifically the neighborhoods of Kamppi, Punavuori, Töölö (South, not North), Kruununhaka, Ullanlinna, and Eira. Sorry, Sörnäinen.

Finland's capital, Helsinki, is a beautiful medium-sized city of about six hundred thousand inhabitants, situated right along the seaside. With roughly three-hundred and thirty islands peppered around the city, it makes for some gorgeous landscapes on the water, and freezing cold winds in the winter.

Upon arriving at Helsinki-Vantaa airport, you'll make it through the terminal in no time—it will be the fastest airport in Europe you'll ever experience! However, since there are no train connections to and from the airport, you'll take a bus, making it the slowest airport journey of your life.

At least Helsinki has no traffic.

Or you can take a taxi. A very expensive taxi. It's 7.30€ just to get in the taxi. But you'll be entering a very nice taxi, most likely a Mercedes with leather seats. A sullen Finn wearing a tie will help you with your luggage, and even open the door for you! Wow, did you just land in Beverly Hills?! He'll then take you directly to your destination while driving at a safe speed without any annoying chit-chat. You can focus on what matters the most: Updating your Foursquare location. Best of all? The driver will happily take your Diner's Club card as payment! Diner's Club! (NOTE: If you asked the driver to take you to the Old Town, he'll drop you off at Tallinn ferry – that leads to Helsinki's Old Town).

@philschwarzmann – The ferry from Tallinn is a museum of old laptops and ancient Nokia phones. I pulled out my iPad – passengers think I'm from the future!

The Helsinki Metropolitan area is made up of over a million people. It's divided up by three beltways, sometimes called "ring roads". Here's how a Helsinki native would describe each ring:

RING I, the innermost ring, divides the city from the countryside. Anyone who is anyone lives within Ring I.

RING II, the middle ring, isn't a ring at all, but more of a "shortest-highway ever". Cars will have the ability to fly by the time this beltway is complete.

RING III is the outermost ring, it divides the countryside from unchartered wilderness.

If you're too poor to live in one of the choice downtown neighborhoods, or you're a farmer, here are some other options around Helsinki:

KALLIO: Once known as a neighborhood for the working class, and childhood home to President Tarja Halonen, Kallio is now for students, hipsters, alcoholics, and Asian handjob artists. As beer is notoriously cheap here the area attracts the drunkest of karaoke singers. When visiting Kallio, be sure to enjoy some free bread at the soup kitchens. Arrive early, the lines are long.

LAUTTASAARI: A rather large island on the southwest side of Helsinki, this community of apartments, small children, and divorcees might as well be part of Espoo.

JAKOMÄKI: Hands down the roughest neighborhood in Helsinki. Unemployment is well over 110 percent. It's so tough, little old ladies feed birds—right in front of the "Don't feed the birds!" signs. It's so ghetto, half the population has been busted—for not paying their TV license! It's so gangsta that people get robbed daily—of their open wifi internet connections! It's so roughneck, a house was raided and the police found an entire room—full of illegally downloaded movies! Let's just say, if Jakomäki was a neighborhood in Detroit – it would be the cleanest, friendliest, and safest neighborhood in all of Detroit.

KÄPYLÄ: This hipster neighborhood is supposedly home to artists, musicians, and socialists. But what's hip about graffiti and R-Kioski's?

RUOHOLAHTI: A freshly-built, concrete neighborhood completely devoid of all culture, beauty, and life. You may call this boring, but wealthy executives from abroad call this home.

EAST HELSINKI: Anywhere east of Kulosaari (including Kulosaari) is for people who want to say they live in Helsinki, but not actually live in Helsinki. It's so far away from the downtown area, this might as well be a separate city.

LEHTISAARI, KULOSAARI, AND KASKISAARI: Three posh islands on the west side of Helsinki with a disproportionate amount of Swedish surnames—these islands are not for you.

What About Espoo?

Espoo is Finland's second largest "city". Why in quotes? Bordering the west side of Helsinki, Espoo is more of a sprawling suburb. It has everything the upper-middle class needs: Shopping malls, plenty of day care, lawns for BBQs, highways, wide parking spots for SUVs, an IKEA, and a Stockmann.

There are no restaurants, so you won't be tempted to take your wife out on a date. There's no culture, so you won't be tempted to leave your oversized house on the weekends. There are no bars, so you won't be tempted to have drinks after work. Instead you'll come right home to your wife, 1.87 kids, and Labrador Retriever. It's the closest thing to American suburbia that you can find in Finland!

@philschwarzmann – I like to go to IKEA, sit on their couches,
then yell at people to 'get the hell out of my living room'.

Some call it heaven, others, hell. It all depends on what
stage you are in life. If you're not sure where you fit in, take
this simple test to see if Espoo is right for you:

1) Are you over thirty? Or, are you over twenty-five and
   crazy enough to want kids already?

   YES ☐ NO ☐

2) Are you married, common-law, or in any other despon-
   dent, long term relationship?

   YES ☐ NO ☐

3) Would an Audi A4 station wagon make you very happy?

   YES ☐ NO ☐

4) If you bought an Audi A4, and then your neighbor
   bought an Audi A6 – would you be very jealous, look up
   their tax records, and then slash their tires?

   YES ☐ NO ☐

5) Do you know what Nordic Walking is?

   YES ☐ NO ☐

6) Mowing lawns, shoveling snow, and renovating houses
   are manly things that a manly man does?

   YES ☐ NO ☐

7) Do you think that playing Farmville is a great way to kill a weekend?

YES ☐ NO ☐

8) Is the #1 goal in your life to become a Vice President at your place of employment?

YES ☐ NO ☐

9) On Saturdays, are you excited that you can go grocery shopping in sweatpants and don't have to wear makeup?

YES ☐ NO ☐

10) Have you given up on most of your hopes and dreams?

YES ☐ NO ☐

Count how many times you said YES to the questions above and match it to the corresponding choices below.

0 You're not ready for Espoo, but might be soon. Take this test again in six months.

1 You're ready for Espoo! Give the landlord your two months notice, and go buy that overpriced townhouse! TIP: Buy a fixer-upper and spend your vacation time renovating. Hello, savings!!

2 You probably already live in Espoo.

3+ You're already dead inside. Years of living in Espoo have made you an empty husk of a human being. They don't call their hockey team the "Espoo Blues" for nothing.

@philschwarzmann – There are two seasons in
Finland: Summer tires, and winter tires.

What's With the "Vantaa" in "Helsinki-Vantaa"?

If you ask a Helsinki resident where they live, they'll proudly say, "Helsingissä!" If you ask an Espoo resident where they live, they'll proudly say, "Espoossa!" If you ask a Vantaa resident where they live, their head drops and shoulders slouch as they reply, "Vitun Vantaalla!".

Vantaa is a suburb to the north of Helsinki and is technically Finland's fourth largest "city". Again with the quotation marks. It's similar to Espoo, except there's even less culture and less Audi A4s, but more bars as well as a shopping mall named "Jumbo" which describes the girth of their patrons' posteriors.

"But if we move to Vantaa, we could get twenty extra square meters for the same price!!" she says. Yes yes, housing sure is cheap next to airports.

@philschwarzmann – All Finnish cities are "Summer cities", they're better in summertime. Vantaa is a "Winter city", it's better covered in the dark.

But I Hate People!

You move to Finland to get away from people. You move to Finnish countryside to REALLY get away from people. Finland is so big and spacious, there's no better place in the world to be if you love forests and high-speed internet connections.

If Helsinki is too much of a bustling metropolis for you, here are a few alternative "cities" for you:

PORVOO – It's a Swedish-speaking seaside town with cobblestone streets! Porvoo residents will claim it only takes them fifteen minutes to get to downtown Helsinki. Don't believe them! They're liars.

LOHJA – Again, "fifteen minutes to downtown"...liars!

TAMPERE – Known for its "black sausage" and jealousy towards Turku natives, Tampere was the capital of red Finland during the Finnish civil war and is a current socialist enclave. Nicknamed "The Manchester of Finland", Tampere locals are equally proud of their lack-of-internationality as well as their lack of proper dress skills. With brick factories, a passion for hockey and mullets, it's the capital of hillbilly Finland.

TURKU – Known for a river and snootiness towards Tampere natives, Turku was once the capital of Finland and is the fifth largest city in the country. Even with an international flair and famous cathedral, Turku might be the most boring city in Finland.

OULU – If this city weren't bad enough, the papermill makes it smell terrible.

ROVANIEMI – Do you really really, *really* hate people?

KUOPIO – Its claim to fame is "kalakukko", a loaf of bread with fish baked inside. Sounds delicious!

JYVÄSKYLÄ – There are no foreigners here, because no foreign person could possibly pronounce the name.

HOW TO SURVIVE A FINNISH WINTER

If lack of employment doesn't send you back to your home-land, the Finnish winters will. While many countries have nice climates with a spell of bad conditions in the winter, Finland has bad weather with a spell of good days in the summer.

Finnish summers are pure heaven. There is no better place to be on the planet than Finland on a warm summer day. Enjoy a picnic in the park, hike through the woods, sun-bathe by the beach, or drink a Lapin Kulta on a terrace – the entire populace is in good spirits during the summer months. You'll need to relax and gather up your strength, cause a long winter is just around the corner.

If Mari is smart, and we know she is cause of Finland's high education standards, she first brought you to Finland in July when summer is at its peak. Let's take you through your first year in Finland:

JULY

The pinnacle of a Finnish summer. The city streets are silent as the entire population is either on holiday or at a summer cottage. At a beach party, you will witness the sun go down then come right back up without setting! COOL!! You should tell your friends on Facebook about this. Could Finland be heaven on earth? It may be! The evenings are a bit warm and only wealthy Finns have air-conditioning, but making love to Mari three times a day puts you right to sleep.

WHAT YOU NEED TO SURVIVE: An oscillating fan.

AUGUST

The jewel of Finland lies in a Finnish forest, so Mari takes you up north to her family's summer cabin. She takes care of all the cooking, cleaning, and sauna preparations while making sure a cold beer is always in your hands. The sun's glimmer off the lake is hypnotizing. Wearing pants and a jacket in the summer is a bit strange though, and shitting in an outhouse wouldn't be so bad if it wasn't for the audience of mosquitos around your private parts. Still, Mari kisses each of your bug bites before bedtime.

WHAT YOU NEED TO SURVIVE: Bug spray.

SEPTEMBER

September 1st arrives and the temperature instantly drops— summer is quickly over, but you refuse to pack away your cargo shorts and Birkenstocks. "It SHOULD be warm out!" The daylight diminishes each day, the leaves begin turning brown, and all the Finns are back to work. Long walks through the woods with Mari are nice, followed by television in the evening. "The Bachelor" is on! Of course they aired this season last year around the rest of the world so you and the rest of the internet already know the ending. But don't spoil it for Mari!

WHAT YOU NEED TO SURVIVE: A flat-screen TV.

OCTOBER

Autumn is in full effect and you've already dived into your "winter clothes". By the middle of the month, all the leaves have fallen and Finland has had its first snow. Winter wonderland! Skype home to your family (cause they'll NEVER call you, as you were the one who left home) and tell them about the beautiful snow—they'll tell you about the backyard BBQ they're having in the summer-like weather. So this is what homesickness feels like? Mari cheers up your spirits by making your new favorite…makaronilaatikko! Yummy!

WHAT YOU NEED TO SURVIVE: A pair of Nokian rubber boots.

NOVEMBER

The days are dark, the temperature is a hair above freezing and it rains everyday. Finland has turned to a brownish-grey hue. A Finn's disposition seems to match their current surroundings. You're ready for bed by about 3pm. Downing a few beers in the evening makes you forget about the outdoors. You do a taste test of all the Finnish beers – the verdict is in: They all taste identical. Mari teaches you how to wear a scarf properly—wow these things are useful!

WHAT YOU NEED TO SURVIVE: A beer home-brewing kit.

DECEMBER

That "summer car" you and Mari bought is now a "winter car". After about ten near-death experiences, you finally get around to changing to winter tires…in the ice. Four hours later, you wash the car and can't get the doors open—they're frozen shut. Five hours later, Mari's younger brother comes to your rescue. But it's Christmas time in Finland! There's snow! Of course, it disappears on Christmas day only to return just after.

WHAT YOU NEED TO SURVIVE: Car lock de-icer spray

@philschwarzmann – I'm too poor to keep my tires
in a tire hotel. Mine stay in a tire motel.

JANUARY

The snow is here to stay, so it's time for winter sports! Finns essentially skied out of the womb, so your skills have some catching up to do. You get outfitted in full cross-country skiing gear and, on your first day out, you soon realize that skiing SUCKS! This isn't fun, this is exercise. It doesn't help that you constantly fall over...on completely flat ground... as four-year-olds whiz by. Mari reminds you that the sun shines longer each day. You brag to your friends back home that it reached −15°C (5F).

WHAT YOU NEED TO SURVIVE: A gym membership.

@philschwarzmann – Can't wait to read some
Wikileaks cables between Finland and the United States.
"TOP SECRET: It's friggin' cold here, send us home. –Bruce"

FEBRUARY

Finnish winters sure are long! You've forgotten what it's like for it to be warm outside. The skin complexion of your stomach matches that of your butt, which matches the color of snow. Time for a winter holiday! The smart decision would be to go someplace warm—but you decide on skiing up north. Maybe swishing down hills will be more enthralling than cross-country? It's not. −25°C (−13F) is no holiday. Mari teaches you her favorite board game: Afrikan Tähti. She wins cause the Star of Africa token is still chocolate-stained from her childhood. You Wikipedia the word "depression".

WHAT YOU NEED TO SURVIVE: 9 cups of coffee each morning.

@philschwarzmann – Does winter make you depressed?
Or is it the fact that sunshine and happiness are just
a plane ticket away…yet you're not there?

MARCH

Winter is still here, with little sign of letting up! This is
getting ridiculous. The rest of Europe is enjoying spring-
like weather—every time a Finnish friend says, "Spring is
here!" you want to punch them. You haven't seen concrete in
months—ice skates would be more appropriate footwear for
the streets of Helsinki at this point. So this is what depression feels like? The days are getting slightly brighter, and
Mari reminds you that warm weather is just around the
corner—can you survive until then?

WHAT YOU NEED TO SURVIVE: Seroquel, 800mg tablets, once per
day.

@philschwarzmann – Only in Finland do you say
"plus" before reading the temperature.

APRIL

What the fuck!? Snow is still everywhere! It's inhumane.
You're going mad. Finland's high suicide rate no longer
puzzles you. It's +3°C (37F) outside and young girls in mini-
skirts are drinking beers on the terrace. The sun doesn't set
till 11pm, but that's just more hours of the day you're forced
to see snow. Mari reminds you not walk on the thinning ice.
Maybe it's a good time to take up ice-fishing?

WHAT YOU NEED TO SURVIVE: A plane ticket home.

MAY

Finally, the snow has melted, except for the occasional left-over snow drift. Finland has already had some +10°C (50F) days. Plants begin to bloom, trees begin to bud. Gravel in the street has been removed, and your summer tires are back on. You're pretty sure you live near a nuclear power plant as all the local rabbits are gargantuan in size. Mari says it's time for "spring cleaning"—your job is to wash all the windows. You wonder if all this scrubbing will help you shed those 5 kilos you gained this winter?

WHAT YOU NEED TO SURVIVE: A cheap bicycle that no one will steal.

@philschwarzmann – It's asparagus season, so you
know what that means...SMELLY URINE!!

JUNE

Summer is here! Of course it feels more like spring as it rains just about every day and you're still wearing a jacket. The sun is out 24/7, keeping you wide awake until 2am and totally messing with your sleeping habits. An entire year has passed. You wonder if you could survive another year in Finland and ask yourself if it gets easier each year?

WHAT YOU NEED TO SURVIVE: A girlfriend from a much warmer climate.

HOW TO BUILD YOUR OWN HOUSE LIKE A REAL FINNISH MAN

All Finns know that a real Finnish man builds his own house. And not like he hires a team to build it for him—no, he spends his nights and weekends actually up there on the roof nailing things together. He's allowed to have help, but they must be family members—and one poorly paid Estonian guy named Kalev.

Upon arrival in Finland you'll be disappointed to see that houses are not the pointy, triangle-shaped Alp chalets you had pictured in your mind. Finnish houses come in two varieties:

"Old-timey country house": This is what a real Finnish man builds. Every time you enter this house you can pretend you live in the forest beside a lake in the nineteenth century. Be sure to paint it some ridiculous color like yellow or pink— your wife wants it to look like her childhood dollhouse.

"Lifeless concrete, metal, and glass block": This is what Finnish architects build. It's "functional". Like Finland isn't depressing enough during winter-tire season, you'd think the local architects would liven up the place, rather than meld homes into the desolate landscape to appear as though they're from a dystrophic science fiction novel.

Constructing a house from scratch goes beyond the limitations of this book (you may want to take a house-building course in the evenings, or rent a house-building instructional DVD), but here's a list of five things you'll find in every Finnish home, and five things you'll never find...

5 Things You'll Find in Every Finnish Home:

ARABIA DISHWARE: Every Finnish woman knows what specific set she's collecting, and the specific sets of her family and female friends. This comes in handy during birthdays and Christmas—you can never have too many coffee saucers. And where there's glassware, you can bet the little sticker is still on it.

AALTO VASE: This lake-shaped vase, designed by famous Finnish designer Alvar Aalto, comes in many sizes and is mandatory in every Finnish household. Even left empty on a shelf, it demonstrates class.

TINY TRASHCAN UNDER THE SINK: Finnish houses are tiny and the kitchen is even smaller. Women can't be wasting precious floor space with a stand-alone trashcan. So they purchase a tiny trashcan, hide it under the sink, then yell at their husband for not emptying it twice a day as is required.

PILE OF SHOES BY THE DOOR: There is no bigger sin in a Finnish household than to walk inside with your shoes on. No one knows exactly how upset a Finnish woman would get if someone did this, cause it's NEVER happened. Finnish streets are so full of dirt, gravel, snow, urine, and puke that it would be sacrilegious to bring that into the house. So upon entering a house, just throw your Puma's on the ever-growing mountain of shoes and pray you don't have stinky feet.

MÖLKKY: This is the greatest lawn game ever and whoever is the first to mass distribute it to the world will become a millionaire. You and an unlimited number of players throw a wood stick at other wood sticks for points. Best of all, you can play this with a beer in hand. No Finnish house or summer cabin is without it. It should be an Olympic sport. The Finns would get a silver medal.

5 Things You Won't Find in a Finnish Home

SPACE: Finns live in some of the smallest homes in Europe. The smaller the home, the easier it is to heat—and that's important if it's the eighteenth century. It's typical for a family of four to live in 80sq/m. Children share rooms, parents have little space for themselves. Cellars are rare, so closet space is utilized well. The father's "den" is often the pub on the corner.

@philschwarzmann – Every house in Finland has a sauna! We'd rather have a spare bedroom.

WALL-TO-WALL CARPETING: Even the idea of wall-to-wall carpeting makes Finns sick to their stomach. How does it ever get properly cleaned? How can you take it outside to beat it? All Finns know that a rug is only thoroughly cleaned when it's taken outside, rubbed in fresh snow, then hung and beaten with a giant, tennis racket-like fly swatter.

A BATHTUB OR SHOWER STALL: A Finnish bathroom is essentially one giant bathtub, the entire space is waterproof. Finns will never know the joys of a rubber ducky.

A DRYER: If you want your neon-colored tracksuit to last you thirty years like it should, you can't put it in a harsh dryer. Plus, dryers take up precious space! Use multiple drying racks instead, they take up even more space.

A SWIMMING POOL: LOL! There's already a skating rink down the street, who needs their own private rink?

HOW TO GET FAMOUS IN FINLAND

The tiny nation of Finland, with its 5.4 million people, seems to have the same number of celebrities as a 300 million-person country. That's thanks to the plethora of yellow press news rags that rule the media. While the tabloid press in other countries are skeptically observed, Finland's are treated as matter-of-fact. If you appear on the front page of *Seiska,* congratulations, you're famous in Finland.

Getting famous may be a dream in larger countries, but it's an easy reality in Finland. Every Finn knows someone famous. Seriously. Ask a Finn right now. They either went to high school with a famous person, or a famous person lives in their building. And there's a 12 percent chance the person you asked is famous themselves.

If your lifelong dream is to become the mockery of an entire nation, err, to get famous—you chose the right country. What will you do to get on page 17 of *Hymy*? Let's have a look at some of Finland's starlets for advice...

SUSAN RUUSUNEN: Simply sleep with someone famous. Like the Prime Minister. Then write a book about it and appear half-naked in tabloids.

TANJA KARPELA: Win Miss Finland, become the Minister of Culture and change boyfriends every other day.

NEIL HARDWICK: Migrate to Finland and write some of the country's best comedy, but find your legacy based on the burn out you had years later.

JOHANNA TUKIAINEN – Get the Minister of Foreign Affairs to send you sexy text messages.

PAUL WESTLAKE – Be the only well-known English textbook author in the world.

KIMMO WILSKA – Pretend to drink beer during a news broadcast.

GEORGE GAYNES – Star as Commandant Eric Lassard in *Police Academy*.

LINUS TORVALDS – Design the world's most popular unused operating system.

MAILA NURMI – Create "Vampira" and star in the worst film of all time.

TOM OF FINLAND – Become the world's most recognized gay caricature.

TARJA HALONEN – Look exactly like Conan O'Brien.

MATTI NYKÄNEN – Win an Olympic gold medal in the "Drinking" competition.

TONY HALME – Become a WWF wrestler, then call the president a lesbian.

JUSSI HALLA-AHO – Author a blog that leads you to being convicted of "inciting racial hatred" then become a member of parliament thanks to it.

HARRY HARKIMO – Prove that deep pockets, not good looks, gets you beautiful women.

MARKKU FROM FINLAND – Become an internet sensation.

WHY SWEDISH-SPEAKING FINNS ARE BETTER PEOPLE THAN FINNISH-SPEAKING FINNS

Roughly five percent of Finns are native Swedish speakers known as the "Swedish Finns", or confusingly, "Finnish Swedes", or more accurately, "Swedish-speaking Finns", or Swedishly, "finlandssvenskar", or Finnishly, "pappa betalar".

You'll find most of them located on the southern and western coasts of Finland. While most are bilingual, speaking both Swedish and Finnish, you will find a few hillbillies up north who only learned Swedish and essentially quarantined themselves off to a very small part of the country.

They have their own political party that gets roughly five percent of the vote during elections. They even created their own flag (it's identical to the Finnish flag, but with a bright red background and IKEA-yellow cross). They have their own semi-autonomous islands, the Åland Islands, located southwest of Finland, and much closer to Sweden. Rumor says when all good Swedish-Finns die they go to Åland, or "Finlandssvenskar heaven"—it's kinda like South Florida for American Jews.

But, to the point: Swedish-speakers are far superior to the Finnish-speakers in every way imaginable—they're wealthier, more educated, more cultured, more sophisticated, more international, they have better social skills, better clothes, better looks, a much better language, they don't get drunk, they all drive fancy cars, they all have boats, they all have summer cottages in the archipelago for their boats, their language is pleasing to the ear, they throw crayfish parties in the summer and drink schnapps, their language doesn't sound like robotic drone from the 1950s, and all the great Finns in Finnish history have Swedish names.

And here are some nasty stereotypes Finns say about the Swedish-Finns: they're snobs, they think they're better than everyone, they're gay, they're Swedish, they don't allow Finnish-speakers into their cliques, they don't give jobs to Finnish-speakers, they control all the power in Finland, they force people to learn Swedish, they have an easier time getting into schools because the requirements aren't as hard, they're loud, they sing stupid songs in unison at pubs, they bribed Google Maps to display only Swedish city and road names, handball is lame.

There's probably no bigger taboo in Finland than the relationship between the Finnish speakers and Swedish speakers. You'll never see this animosity discussed publicly. When the two groups are together they won't say anything mean, but get them each alone and they'll make catty comments about each other.

WHICH POLITICAL PARTY SHOULD I JOIN?

With eight political parties in parliament and many obscure smaller parties, choosing a political party can be overwhelming—especially since the differences between each are so minute. Here's a quick run-down of each party to help you decide...

NATIONAL COALITION PARTY (Kokoomus): These conservatives promise to lower your taxes! With some of the highest taxes in the world, you'll quickly come to realize that these people have done nothing for decades.

CENTRE PARTY (Keskusta): Do you live on a farm? Do you enjoy small town life? Do you distrust the EU? Then the Centre Party is for you, redneck! Life was certainly better when we all milked cows for a living, wasn't it?

SOCIAL DEMOCRATS (SDP): Lenin, Guevara, and Marx were all great thinkers, weren't they? If you answered "yes" to that question, than the Social Democrats are for you, comrade. Now shorten those work weeks and wonder why you don't get paid enough. Strike!!

SWEDISH PEOPLE'S PARTY (RKP): Is Swedish your mother tongue? 'Nuff said, this party is yours. Amazing how everyone who speaks the same language is expected to share the same political beliefs.

TRUE FINNS (Perussuomalaiset): Foreigners are the root of all evil. Aren't they?

@philschwarzmann – Perussuomalaiset would love to tell us
foreigners to "PISS OFF!" But they can't. They don't speak English.

CHRISTIAN DEMOCRATS (KD): Do you have a special relationship
with Jesus? Do you hate gays, even though your cousin
probably is one? And do you live out in the middle of nowhere
because the devil resides in both large cities and TV sets?
Hallelujah you've found your party!

GREEN PARTY (Vihreät): Are you young, idealistic and fanatical
about mother Earth? Then come share a joint with these
hippies. Peace.

LEFT ALLIANCE (Vasemistoliitto): But what about all the good
things the Soviet Union did?

STORY: I got to see an early screening of the movie "TRON". They
asked everyone to hand over their camera phones to prevent
any illegal filming. I said I didn't have a camera phone. They
thanked me and handed me free popcorn and soda.

3 FINLAND? FUNLAND!

HOW DRUNK CAN I GET ON FINNISH HOLIDAYS?

Finns don't exactly go overboard with traditions. Sure, Finland has traditions like everywhere else, they're just not held as sacred. Forget Mother's Day, sleep through May Day, or tell your family you need to "work" during Christmas...no one will care. The only ones who may care are the friends you promised to go get hammered with—cause Finnish holidays are just an excuse to get drunk on a Tuesday.

@philschwarzmann – For the sake of warmer weather, let's move May Day to June. Then from June to July.

But what level of drunkenness is acceptable for each holiday? You certainly don't want to be heaving on Johan Vilhelm Snellman's flag day, or even worse, only be a bit tipsy on your workmate's 26th birthday. The guide below will explain each important holiday and is accompanied by a British euphemism to describe the level of drunkenness you can achieve.

Finnish Independence Day (Itsenäisyyspäivä)
December 6th

Finland's Independence Day is a very solemn, commemorative, and ceremonial day. Finns stay at home, have a sauna, visit loved ones at the graveyard, light candles, and drink glögi. Since Finland's independence is so recent (1917), there are still many Finns who remember Russia's rule, and a few veterans who fought during that war. Soon the last of them will have passed...and Finnish Independence Day can finally be fun!! Break out the hamburgers and hotdogs, let's move this party to July!

But until then, Finns will spend the evening sitting in front of the television watching the Independence Day Ball at the President's "Palace" (if you've seen the "palace" you'll know why it's in quotes). Each year, the President invites Finland's politicians, diplomats, and cultural elite—and those who are currently sleeping with them—to a night of drinking and dancing.

All of Finland ridicules each guest's dress as they enter the "palace" atrium to shake hands with the President. Who will be the best dressed? Who the worst dressed? Oh that dress is hideous! Why did she pick those colors? Why would she show that nasty tattoo? She looks like a total slut! Who's that ugly guy she's with this year? ...so many questions – just for Tanja Karpela

LEVEL OF DRUNKENNESS: Slighty squiffy

Little Christmas (Pikkujoulu)
Begins earlier every year, by 2030 it will begin in August

It's the kickoff of the Christmas season, usually commencing at the end of November or beginning of December. Pikkujoulu is often your typical office Christmas party, the one day of the year when you can get wasted, slap your boss, and make inappropriate advances at your female colleagues without getting fired. The day after Pikkujoulu is an unofficial day off, as most people are attending their first couples therapy session.

LEVEL OF DRUNKENNESS: Totally off ye' pickle trolley

Christmas
December 24th, 25th, and 26th

Finns believe that the rest of the world is mistaken—all Finns know that Santa Claus is actually from northern Finland. With all of it's great welfare benefits, Finland is the perfect home if you're out of work 355 days a year like Santa.

Finnish Christmas is another solemn, peaceful, and ceremonial holiday. You drink glögi, eat ham, decorate the Christmas tree, visit graveyards, and write letters to Santa (just a single local stamp required). And no need to put up Christmas lights outside your house, In Finland you'll leave them up year round! Here they are called "winter lights"—in other parts of the world, they are called "trailer trash".

In Finland, you do everything any normal Christian country would do except go to church. Only wacky religious nutters go to church on Christmas.

Finnish parents hire a part time Santa to visit their houses on Christmas Eve. These Santas usually arrive intoxicated. Santa's helpers work one day a year and can't even show up sober for that. The Santa Clauses advertise themselves in the local Finnish newspapers as "raitis pukki" (sober santa) to verify they'll arrive sober. Otherwise it's assumed Santa will show up drunk—but you will get a much more affordable Santa. And if you're the type to pinch pennies on a Santa Claus for your kids, you won't mind if he's inebriated, cause you're probably drunk yourself.

The Santa Claus of Finland is not the plump, jolly, red suited Santa the Coca-Cola people would like you to believe. Finnish Santa is frightening! He walks slowly, talks slowly, and carries a big stick. Before the children receive gifts, they first must sing songs and prove they've been good. For little Finnish children, it's both the happiest day of their lives as well as the most traumatizing.

LEVEL OF DRUNKENNESS: Gleefully goosed
LEVEL OF DRUNKENNESS FOR SANTA: Merrily mullered

New Year's
December 31st & January 1st

If you've ever wondered what it's like to be in the middle of an air raid, simply stand outside at midnight on New Year's Eve in any Finnish town, and watch as you're engulfed in a swell of bottle rockets and M80's – it will trump any "professional" fireworks show you've ever seen. Pop open a few bottles of bubbly and kick off the New Year with a hangover. Your New Year's resolution to "drink less" begins tomorrow.

LEVEL OF DRUNKENNESS: Cabbaged and clobbered

Feast of the Epiphany
January 6th

No one knows why this is a bank holiday but everyone has off work. It is the day to take down your Christmas tree and sip on some wine.

LEVEL OF DRUNKENNESS: Had a couple of shickers

Valentine's Day
February something...

If there's one day of the year you don't want to be drunk, it's Valentine's Day, or "Friendship Day" as the Finns call it. While an American greeting card influence has slowly crept onto Finnish soil, no Finnish woman expects diamonds on Friendship Day. Finnish men won't bother to buy gifts or chocolates, so order roses and make all of Mari's co-workers jealous. Don't be surprised if the florist doesn't know what a "dozen" is—Finnish flowers come in groups of ten—the metric system is so romantic. And it's not like a "dozen" would get a you a discount anyways, this is Finland, they'll just multiple the price of one rose by twelve.

LEVEL OF DRUNKENNESS: Break out the bubbly

St. Patrick's Day
March 17

Every European city has an Irish pub. Walk into any one of them and find the exact same thing: warm ale, fatty foods, dim lights, old signs on the wall, terrible music, bad jokes, wood everything, and all the local idiot expats—in Finland it's no exception. If anyone can drink like the Irish, it's the Finns.

LEVEL OF DRUNKENNESS: Langered and locked out of your mind

Easter
It's a mystery every year

Four-day weekend! Jesus should have been crucified more often. The snow has finally melted (hopefully), the weather is getting warmer (possibly), and Spring is in the air! (along with the smell of thawing dog poo) Finns often retreat to the countryside and prepare their cabins for summer.

@philschwarzmann – Everyone knows the
Easter Bunny is from Northern Finland.

On Palm Sunday, the Sunday before Easter, children dress up like witches and go door-to-door exchanging twigs and song for candy—it's some sort of twisted mix between Halloween and *The Wizard of Oz*.

LEVEL OF DRUNKENNESS: Wobbly

@philschwarzmann – Similar to Jesus, I can turn wine into urine.

May Day (Vappu)
May 1

Vappu is two great days of drinking rolled into one. On the evening of April 31st, Finland's youth binge until the wee hours of the morning. If you graduated from "lukio" (university-bound high school), you'll strut around in your graduation cap. The caps are white and very official-looking —it's the one day a year people in the Navy can pretend they graduated high school.

@philschwarzmann – American high school students throw their graduation caps into their air and never see them again. Finns keep them on until they DIE.

May 1st is a bank holiday and day for drunks and families alike. As a carnival of sorts, families spend time outside to enjoy the spring air, admire some festive balloons, and have a nice brunch. For students it's day two of binge drinking. In Helsinki, young people flock to the city's southern-most park, Kaivopuisto, for the country's largest picnic—followed by the country's largest hangover.

LEVEL OF DRUNKENNESS: Nicely irrigated with a horizontal lubricant

---

@philschwarzmann – Finns always say that American high schools are so easy. Bullshit! In Baltimore City Public Schools, only one-third graduate – it's hard!

Eurovision Song Contest
May

Each year, all of Europe (and Israel) take part in a song contest. Finns often get together for house parties, sit in front of the television and watch Finland battle for last place. (Unless it's 2006, when Finland won with the ultimate Eurovision gimmick to date.)

LEVEL OF DRUNKENNESS: Hard Rock Hammer-blowed

Finland wins ice-hockey world championships
1995 & 2011

Any Finnish sporting event is a reason to get wankered, but if Finland makes it to the annual ice-hockey world championship finals—win or lose, you're getting pissed.

LEVEL OF DRUNKENNES: Boarded and leveled

@philschwarzmann – Looking forward to some ice hockey world championships! Division III, Mongolia vs. Luxembourg, baby!!

Ascension Day (Helatorstai)
Thursday, 39 days after Easter Sunday

Another holiday when Finns say, "We have off tomorrow? Why? Oh, that's right...Jesus. Sure, why not! Thanks, JC!"

LEVEL OF DRUNKENNESS: Bright eyed and bushy tailed

Midsummer (Juhannus)
Late June

The lightest day of the year, and official kickoff to the summer! It's time to visit the summer cabin, have a beer, enjoy a daytime sauna, swim in a freezing cold lake, crack open another beer, get back in the sauna, dive in the ice cold lake, drink ten more beers, and finally roll around naked in the flowers. If you take an inebriated boat ride into the lake, be sure to urinate while standing, and be one of the dozens who drown each Midsummer in boat-urinating accidents. It's a Juhannus tradition!

LEVEL OF DRUNKENNESS: Blootered, blottoed, and bluttered

Bachelor Parties & Hen Nights
4–6 months after she's pregnant

Finnish women dress the bride-to-be in something ridiculous then parade her around town. Finnish men must do hard labor for the friends. One thing's for sure, it's a night of fun and heavy boozing.

MEN'S LEVEL OF DRUNKENNESS: Smashed
WOMEN'S LEVEL OF DRUNKENNESS: Sloshed

Weddings
Usually summer

Put on the nicest pair of khakis and that tie your wife bought you twenty years ago, it's time for a countryside wedding! Hide the alcohol in the trunk of your car, you don't want the pastor to see it.

LEVEL OF DRUNKENNESS: Drunk as a Lord

A Night of the Arts
Late August

When you think of a modern art festival, what comes to mind? If you think, "Let's get pissed!" congratulations, you're a Finn.

LEVEL OF DRUNKENNESS: Loo la

All Saints Day (Halloween)
Early November

The American Halloween tradition has made it to Finland. While trick-or-treating is left for Easter, Finland's young adults wear costumes and attend parties. Finnish women dress in a wide variety of costumes such as: Slutty nurse, slutty vampire, slutty angel, slutty princess, slutty slut, and Lady Gaga.

LEVEL OF DRUNKENNESS: With the fairies

Your Facebook friend's 26th Birthday
Some Monday Night

Some loud-mouthed chick you barely know is celebrating the big 2-6!! She's sent all 849 of her friends on Facebook an invite. Attendance is mandatory! And why shouldn't it be? A birthday is only something everyone gets every single year—unless you were born on a Leap Year, or Christmas. But don't worry, if you can't make her Monday night bash, the next day you'll see Facebook photos of her wearing a tiara.

HER LEVEL OF DRUNKENNESS: Jan hammered

Flag Days
Throughout the Year

What to do on a flag day? Fly the Finnish flag! Flag days are held for important national events like Independence Day and Election Day, while other flag days are poet's birthdays. On one particular Flag Day, you eat a special pastry and go sledding!

LEVEL OF DRUNKENNESS: Straight as an arrow

Your girlfriend's name day
You'll forget

Every Finnish name is attached to a particular day in the calendar (unless your name is "Ridge"). Your friends give you a little gift or at the very least, wish you a Happy Name Day. You'll never remember your girlfriend's name day. But don't worry, she'll remind you...the day after.

LEVEL OF DRUNKENNESS: Square

HOW TO GO OUT ON A FRIDAY NIGHT, FINNISH STYLE

It's Friday night. You haven't had a drink all week, cause only alcoholics drink during the week. It's time to head out on the town! Here's a sample breakdown of a night out in Finland, drink by drink...

1 GLASS SPARKLING	You begin by walking to the party at a friend's apartment in Kallio. People are standing at the crosswalk cause the sign says DON'T WALK, yet there are no cars in sight. Common sense tells you to cross. Everyone follows your example.
2 GLASSES SPARKLING	The place is silent, you think you're the first to arrive, but everyone is just sitting on the floor quietly nursing their beer and listening to Leevi and the Leavings.
1 WARM OLVI	The party is BYOB. The host put out a couple bowls of chips. Not much of a party. You leave.
1 COLD KARHU	You pass a friend on the street and decide to grab some food at a restaurant. The waitress is miserable. She doesn't get tips so she could care less how friendly she is.

2 COLD KARHU'S

It takes you fifteen minutes to pay your check. You could walk out of there without paying and no one would notice or care. The check includes a space for a tip.

You and your friend stop by a nightclub. The doorman is the biggest asshole you've ever met. He's still upset he didn't make it to the NHL 25 years ago and he takes it out on each of his patrons.

The coat check guy wants 2.20€. But you explain, "It's summer, I clearly don't have a coat." He gets aggressive and clearly wants to start a fight. You give him the money.

1 PINOT GRIGIO

After an unfriendly experience walking into the club, it's time to start drinking. You order a glass of wine. The barman asks if you want "small, medium, large". Classy!

2 PINOT GRIGIO'S

You order another glass of wine. A large. The barman asks if you want ice in your glass. Double classy!

1 MOJITO

You order a mojito. When you get the check it includes six different items! You're about to accuse the barman of ripping you off, then you realize those six items are the ingredients of a mojito, each individually priced.

1 JALOVIINA SHOT

You text your girlfriend saying you're on your way home, but then you run into a friend from work. He buys a round of shots. You can't say NO to a shot, that would be rude!

9 JALOVIINA SHOTS

Time for karaoke! Normally you hate karaoke.

?? JALOVIINA SHOTS

It's 4am. The bar is closing. Time for kebab!

5 GLASSES OF WATER

You wake up on your bathroom floor, it's 2pm. You have the worst hangover in your life. You don't remember a thing from last night, but according to your phone you dialed about 13 different friends, including your mom. You're 34 years old, will this behavior ever end? Nah!

HOW TO AVOID SERVING IN THE FINNISH ARMY, EVEN IF YOU'RE GAY

Every male Finnish citizen must join the army before age thirty or else face the consequences. It's 2011, yet the country still fears the Russians could invade at any moment. All this means is that at about age eighteen, fresh out of high school, most Finnish boys leave home for the first time and spend six months running around in the woods shooting fake guns. Finnish women say, "They leave as boys, and come back as men!"

Finns have up until their thirtieth birthday to join or else they're sent to prison. But if you have trouble holding on to slippery soap in the shower, here are some army alternatives...

CIVIL SERVICE: Would you rather sleep with your girlfriend than sleep with boys in tents? Join the civil service, and everyone will say you're "gay" or a "communist"! Instead of six months in the forest, you'll be forced to spend one year performing a meaningless task for the state. Your father will be ashamed of you, your friends will make fun of you, your neighbors will talk behind your back, and your future perspective employers will turn you down from jobs.

BECOME A JEHOVAH'S WITNESS: All other religions must do their civic duty but the Jehovah's Witnesses are immune because violence is against their religion. Do you also believe in non-violence but don't believe in some sort of magical sky daddy who won't wake you from the dead until the Earth is free of sin? Tough luck! But maybe the army is better than knocking on stranger's doors and handing out copies of *The Watchtower*.

DON'T BE FINNISH: If you're a foreigner in Finland and thinking of impressing your friends back home with dual-citizenship...wait until your thirtieth birthday—then you don't need to join the army. It'll take you until you're thirty-years-old anyway to learn Finnish and pass the citizenship exam anyway.

FLEE THE COUNTRY: Definitely the longest alternative. Some have chosen to flee the country for several years hoping that their prison sentence will have expired upon their return. Flee somewhere warm.

DON'T PASS GO, GO DIRECTLY TO JAIL: Finnish prisons aren't so bad. In fact they're some of the finest in the world. There are more freedoms than in North Korea, cooler weather than Afghanistan, and better food than India.

TELL'EM YOU'RE GAY!: Wrong country, that only works in the United States.

STORY: I was heading home from Finnish class in my very first week in Finland. Me, and about fifty other bystanders outside the Tapiola Stockmann witnessed a woman pull down her pants and have a slow bowel-movement at the bus stop. For me, the horrifying action was not the woman taking a shit, it was fifty Finns not doing anything about it. Even worse, they just ignored the situation, pretending like nothing was happening.

4 FOOD & DRUNK

WHAT'S FOR BREAKFAST?

French President Jacques Chirac once said, "After Finland, Britain is the country with the worst food." Ouch!!
Italian Prime Minister Silvio Berclusconi agrees, "I've
been to Finland and I had to endure the Finnish diet..."
Double ouch!! Former Finnish Prime Minister Matti Van-
hanen replied back in defense of Finnish food with, "I like
spaghetti, as long as it is not spiced too much. I like simple
food." Zing!!

What's your favorite Finnish restaurant outside Finland?
Can't name one? Don't worry, no one can, there aren't any.
Finnish cuisine doesn't really exist. Sure there are some
specialties you won't find elsewhere in the world but these
were created out of necessity or durability, rather than taste.
Fish baked into a loaf a bread isn't particularly appetizing,
but it does keep for a long time.

Every Finn knows that a hearty bowl of porridge in
the morning will last you until lunchtime—which is about
10:30—so porridge lasts about two or three hours. Every
Finnish freezer is packed with berries and jams, so toss
these in your porridge if you're into food with flavor.

Even Jared from Subway doesn't eat sandwiches in the
morning, but Finns do. If it's a weekend morning, go for the
open-faced sandwich topped with ham, cheese, cucumber...
and butter. Not mayonnaise, butter. Or substitute the ham
for cold-smoked salmon, then try not to puke.

While you have options on top of the bread, the bread itself
is a standard affair: dark rye. If spinach puts hair on your
chest, then Finnish dark rye hand knits you a wool sweater.
It's hard, dry, and can last for months without spoiling—and
it's completely devoid of all taste. Dark rye is just a vessel for

shoveling cucumber into your gullet and the Finns universally LOVE it. Surprisingly, this fine bread can't be found anywhere outside of Finland, thus it's the number one export to Finns living abroad.

THE COFFEE AND CAKE TRAP

Addiction to illegal drugs may be low in Finland, but addiction to caffeine is the highest in the world. The average person consumes 1.3kg of coffee each year, while in Finland the average person consumes 12kg each year. (Norway comes in a distant second with 9.9kg.) And it's no surprise, Finland's entire day is centered around coffee—it's necessary to stay awake during the long, dark winters. In Finland you'll drink coffee first thing when you wake up, then make multiple trips to the coffee machine throughout the morning, then enjoy coffee after lunch, throughout the afternoon with company (päiväkahviseura), after dinner with desert, at night, and finally, you'll chew on a handful of sleeping pills.

Along with heavy coffee consumption, there's a thing known as the Finnish "coffee and cake trap": You pop in to say "moi!" to your friends. They of course offer you coffee and you of course accept. Cake is served. You sit around chatting, eating, and drinking for so long, that it's meal time. You eat a meal, then have mandatory coffee and cake. You sit around for so long, it's meal time again...Now you're trapped!

LUNCH TIME, THE SECOND BEST PART OF YOUR WORKDAY

Lunch is possibly the most important meal of the day. So important that Finns eat it around 10:30am, when other nationalities are enjoying breakfast. Finns eat huge meals full of fish, meat, stew, potatoes, vegetables, and buttered bread served with milk. Load up on that and then try not to fall asleep.

WHERE'S THE BEEF? DINNER.

After beefing up on carbs at lunch, the Finnish dinner could be a bit smaller. Maybe some leftovers from a previous meal or "boxed" foods (Fish box, Ham box, Macaroni box, Liver box, etc). They're as delicious as they sound.

Now, there are a few rules about Finnish dinnertime you should be aware of:

Make sure your meat is drowning in some sort of fatty, tasteless sauce.

Spices to include: salt, pepper, and that's it.

Try to pile different foods on your fork at once. Take a green bean, a chunk of beef, then dip it all in mashed potatoes—it's like impromptu Finnish sushi.

Food is sacred, don't play with it. But no need to say grace before meals.

If at a special event, take the fish and salad first, then meat second.

Lick up every piece of fat and grease on your plate. And when there's nothing left, take a piece of dark rye bread and twirl it around your plate looking for that last bit of slop—like you're a death row inmate eating his last meal.

Place your utensils in front of you at the 4 o'clock position when finished eating. Otherwise, no one knows you're done.

When leaving the dinner table, as abrupt yet lackadaisical as possible, say "kiitos" to the cook.

@philschwarzmann – If there was a plate-licking contest between a dog and a Finn, the Finn would win.

What's For Dessert?

Finns love dessert: Sweet breads, cinnamon rolls, pastries, cake, pie, chocolate and ice-cream. It's best if it's homemade, don't be lazy and buy that frozen stuff from the store. Keep in mind that Finns like to drop fruit into each dessert! Savory chocolate cake can't be complete with out bananas. Ice cream can't be eaten without berries on top.

Which is Better, Hesburger or McDonald's?

Neither. Go to Carrol's instead.

"HELLO, MY NAME IS FINLAND, AND I'M AN ALCOHOLIC"

Drinking has a bit of a Finland problem. Some say Finland is a nation of alcoholics. That may be true, but it's not their fault—the weather is freezing, the daylight is short, the natives are reserved, the abuse is tolerated, and there's nothing good on TV. That all makes for some pretty heavy drinkers.

When Visiting Finland, What Should I Drink?

Every Finn can fit into one of six different drinking categories. Read below to see which type of Finnish drinker you are, then learn your drink of choice:

The Cognac Connoisseur

Features: Mustache. Huge gut. Loves his Mercedes and gun collection. Hates Russians. Votes Perussuomalaiset (a nationalist political party).

Hobbies: Hunting. Ice-hockey. The News. Racism.

Favorite Song: "Tulvii Pohjanmaa" by Janne Tulkki

Drink of choice: Martell Cordon Bleu Cognac, Expensive Reds, Finnish Beer

The Cognac Connoisseur finishes off every good meal with a glass of cognac. Such class! This simpleton grew up poor, gained wealth in the construction industry, and now impresses women by pretending to be an expert on the wine list. When the waitress pours a glass of wine, the Cognac Connoisseur sniffs it, twirls it, eyes it, sips it, swirls it, and finally, embarrasses himself in front of his guests. When a flight attendant asks,"red or white?", the Cognac Connoisseur sitting in economy asks to see the bottle, lowers his spectacles to examine the bottle, pretends to know French, then accepts.

The Teenage Dachshund-Walker

Features: NY Yankees baseball cap. Ridiculous sunglasses. T-shirt of some fake American college.

Hobbies: Singstar. Drinking in a park. Not studying.

Favorite Song: "Selvä Päivä" by Petri Nygård

Drink of choice: 12-pack of Karhu, cider

These underage drinkers are seen zigzagging across town with a 12-pack, "dachshund", or Karhu beer in hand. If they do stop, it's to urinate on the side of a building. Karhu is the beer choice of teenage boys as it has 4.6 percent alcohol content, 0.1 percent more than Karhu's competitor, Lapin Kulta. Girlfriends of dachshund-walkers drink cider. Finland is so safe that teenage girls can pass out at bus stops and wake up with their purse, shoes, and virginity.

The Yuppie

Features: Black leather man-bag. Leg-hugging skinny jeans. Scarf even though it's warm. Adequacy in the Swedish language.

Hobbies: Travel and cooking.

Favorite Song: "Kärleken Väntar" by Kent.

Drink of Choice: Mojito, Sparkling Wine, Schnaps (with crayfish), Belgian Ale

These liberals complain about Alko's monopoly on the industry, claiming their wide selection could be wider. And they whine about Finland's high prices, even though they can easily afford booze. You'll recognize The Yuppie at Alko, as they're the one looking UP in the wine section, and not kneeling towards the cheap bottles. While most other types of drinkers only get wasted on Friday and Saturday nights, The Yuppies have learned the European art of getting sloshed during the weekday—cause after all, you had a hard day of Facebooking at the office! Treat yourself.

The Pekka

Features: Black clothes. Marlboro Lights. Ilta-Sanomat. Gold "Finnish Lion" chain around neck. Nokia mobile phone.

Hobbies: Fixing Toyotas. Watching Sports. Karaoke.

Favorite Song: "Ulkkometso" by Popeda

Drink of Choice: Jaloviinia, Koskenkorva, Lonkero, the cheapest beer on tap.

These are your classic Finns. They love nothing more than being at the pub. Pekka and Sari are normally very shy and reserved, but after a few long drinks, they're carefree and chatty, even chatty enough to speak English and ask a foreigner how they like Finland. If they do travel, it's to Tallinn to stock up on cheap beer—Finns bring an empty cart to reunite cases of Lapin Kulta "Export" with their homeland. In Finland, as part of a self-inflicted sobriety test, people often stay sober during the entire month of January—Pekka does not.

The Professional

Features: Pink skin. Long beard. Last month's underwear.

Hobbies: Drinking. Collecting bottles.

Favorite Song: Whatever's playing on your boombox in the park.

Drink of Choice: Alcohol. Windshield wiper fluid.

When a fulltime job begins to interfere with your drinking, you need to set your priorities: Go pro! These wastes of human space lurk around larger Finnish cities, harass people, and pass out on public transportation.

STORY: After years of paying out of pocket for an expensive private dentist every six months, I decided to utilize Finland's "free healthcare" and book an appointment with the public dentist. They told me the first available slot was in seven months. Seven! After my appointment the public dentist said I didn't need to return for another five years. Five! It's a miracle! My entire life, dentists have been telling me to come back every six months, but now I only needed to endure a dentist chair's torture once every five years. Thank you, free dentists!

5 HOW TO MARRY A FINNISH GIRL

MARRYING A FINNISH GIRL IN 10 EASY STEPS

Finnish women are the most amazing women in the world. That's not a matter of opinion—that's a fact. They're beautiful and intelligent and determined and devoted and modern and feminine and masculine and down-to-earth and humorous and most importantly...they love foreign men.

Why foreign men? Foreign men have manners and status and social skills and confidence and emotions and passion and thick eyebrows and a different gene pool and exotic surnames like "Jones". But it's not that foreign men are so great, it's that Finnish men are so not-so-great.

While Finnish men are introverted, unable to express themselves, foreign men are extroverts, always quick to tell a Finnish woman how pretty she looks in that dress from H&M.

While Finnish men are dull, from some boring town like Mikkeli, foreign men are exotic, they bring status to the family so the mother-in-law can brag to the neighbors that her daughter is dating an American.

While Finnish men are shy, incapable of approaching a girl without alcohol as his wingman, foreign men are confident, they'll easily violate a Finnish woman's personal space and flirt while inappropriately finessing her elbow.

Marrying a Finnish woman couldn't be easier. But in case you need to speed up the process, like if your cruise ship is only in port for several hours, here's a step-by-step process to locking down your very own Finnish woman...

STEP 1: Understand That Finnish Girls Are Better Than Swedish Girls

First you need to be convinced that you want a Finnish girl specifically. "But aren't Swedish girls better?" Short answer: No. Long answer: Noooooooooooo. Sure your friends and family will be more impressed if their son is dating a "Swedish girl" than a "Finnish girl", but think of it this way—they'll be more impressed if their son is dating a "Finnish girl" than an "Estonian girl". As they say, "beggars can't be choosers".

Below is a list as to why Finnish girls are better than Swedish girls.

On a scale between 1 and 10, Finnish girls are 8's and Swedish girls are 10's

The eternal question: Who is better looking? Finnish girls or Swedish girls? Sweden definitely has more 10's—drop dead gorgeous blondes that bring tears to your eyes. However, those 10's are few and far between, in both countries. In general there exist a fair number of eights in Finland, much moreso than in Sweden. And let's face it, Andrew from Cape Town, will never land a ten in Sweden—he's got a better chance of landing an 8 in Finland. (Or if he were Latino, a 7).

Finnish Girls are Low Maintenance and Swedish Girls are High Maintenance

Finnish girls grew up poor. The majority urinated in an outhouse until they were eleven, while their father traded in their bedroom furniture to pay off his gambling debts. Finnish girls appreciate the simple things in life. Instead of buying jewelry, write her a poem. Instead of a fancy dinner, how about a picnic in the park? Swedish girls grew up wealthy, their daddies traded in their furniture for better IKEA furniture. Your Velcro surfer-wallet can't compete with those high expectations.

Finnish Girls Are Independent While Swedish Girls Will Phone Daddy

There's nothing worse than having to get your father-in-law or brother-in-law to help you. Nothing quite says you're a loser like, "Daddy, can Patrick and I borrow 500 euros?" Swedes have close ties to family. Meanwhile, Finnish women HATE their families, especially their fathers. You and Mari will handle your own problems without the financial support of your in-laws. So go ahead and trade your furniture in for the down payment on that health pill business—it's a gamble that will make you millions!

STEP 2: Single White Finnish Female

So you're convinced that Finnish girls are right for you. Hyvä! Now all you need to do is meet one. If you're in Finland, this should be easy, there are loads of them. But if you're not, there are options as well.

What kind of Finn are you looking for? Carefree student? Mature mother of two? Below are some online personal ads (translated to English) along with the place where you can expect to meet these fine Finnish goddesses.

NAME: Riitta

AD: I'm a forty-five-year old twice-divorcee without any kids, in my custody. I'm 70kg's sober and 50kg's when you're drunk. I'm into spending time with my sister, regretting life decisions, and Friday afternoon hangovers. I'm looking for a man, any man, half my age for a one-night stand and awkward moments in the morning.

WHERE TO FIND ME: Ravintola Kaarle XVIII, Helsinki, Thursday nights

NAME: Janica

AD: I'm a twenty-year old student training to be a flight attendant. There's nothing I love more than travel, sunbathing, and foreign guys with money. I'm searching for an older businessman who can support me, my shopping sprees, and my future teacup poodle.

WHERE TO FIND ME: Aussie Bar, Helsinki, anytime

NAME: Sari

AD: I'm a bitter thirty-seven-year old divorcee with two beautiful children. My ex-husband left us for a much younger woman he met at the Aussie Bar, so I'm a bit out of shape as I've been raising two kids alone. I love my children more than anything, and am looking for a man who is willing to compete with my kids for that love.

WHERE TO FIND ME: Karaoke Bar, drunk, East Helsinki, Friday and Saturday nights

NAME: Hanna

AD: Determined thirty-three-year old workaholic seeks boy toy for fun and procreation. I'm driven by success and my goal in life is to become Vice President of a large multi-national company. I require a handsome man who cooks, cleans, and looks after our future son or daughter in the home I own. While you're confined to the house to work on your "art", I'll be jet-setting to Malaysia having affairs with my colleagues. See my proposal in the attached PowerPoint presentation.

WHERE TO FIND ME: On e-mail, in the hotel bar, or both

NAME: Tarja

AD: Thirty-nine-year old with no kids and a serious case of baby fever. My fiancé of twenty years could never commit, so I finally broke things off. I'm short, blonde, and ovulating. Could you be Mr. Right? If you're desperate and fertile, then you are! Our son will be named Aleksi and daughter Jenna.

WHERE TO FIND ME: On a date.

STEP 3: How To Chat Up a Finnish Girl

There she is. On that couch in the corner, sparkling wine in hand. She could very well be the most beautiful woman you've ever seen. Normally you'd need about fifteen beers to gather the guts to chat with her, but a confidence storms over you. The time is now.

What do you say? How do you act? How do you show that you're cool and witty? Every Finnish girl has been out with a foreign guy. You can't just go up to a Finnish girl and say you're foreign—it's not the Nineties anymore, you're no longer special. So here are a few chat up lines that'll get her giggling...

Could I have your autograph, Miss Finland?

Put your tongue on my flagpole and see if it sticks.

Was that a mosquito that just bit me, or was that love?

When I first saw you, I was like a reindeer in headlights.

Let's go mushroom picking together, cause I'm a fun-gi.

What's your name? I'll write it in the snow with my yellow pen.

Does Finnair have a direct flight from Helsinki to your heart?

Kiss me now, we only have ten minutes to live. The Russians are invading.

Will you marry me? Or am I just (ski-) jumping to conclusions?

You're hot like a sauna.

You're like Koskenkorva, everyone wants a shot.

You're like Lapin Kulta, I want to crack you open.

You're like Karjala, I want to pop off your top.

Let's go ice-fishing, I'll put my rod in your hole.

How about I go sledding into your bedding.

Everyman's right, your bush is a great place to pop a tent.

Everyman's right, I'm gonna deflower your forest.

Do you hunt moose? Cause I hunt beaver.

Like the midnight sun, I'll never leave you.

We're like mustamakkara, we're linked together.

Like mämmi, I'm gonna cover you in cream, sugar.

You're like a snowflake, you're different from all the rest.

You make my balls like the Finnish flag, white and blue.

Do you like to ski? Have you been down my happy trail?

No, that's not a Nokia Communicator in my pocket.

You can make snow angels while standing up.

Do you prefer Finnish Spitz or Finnish swallows?

If Those Lines Don't Work

There is a small minority of Finnish girls who refuse to date foreign guys, most likely due to the language issue. Hard to believe but it's true. They are girls who are very much into the Finnish language (usually musicians, authors, poets, actors, and comics). These ladies simply can't imagine sharing a life with a guy who doesn't share their language. But fear not foreign guys, these "artists" are poor, you don't want to take on their credit card debt. Even if they do strike it big, it's still Finland, they'll always be broke.

STEP 4: The DO's and DON'T's of Dating in Finland

Your cheesy pickup line was so bad, she couldn't help but burst out laughing. You thought she was laughing *with* you and not *at* you, and it gave you the courage to ask her out on a date.

Dating in Finland is a bit of an anomaly. People usually just get drunk at parties, hook up, spend three days in bed together, then move in weeks later. But if you meet a classy gal, here's a list of DOs and DON'Ts when you do land that first date...

DO: Pay the check. The entire check.

Finnish guys split the check, even on the first date! In any other culture, that's like saying to your date, "Well I guess I'm not getting lucky tonight. Bye!" But in Finland, this is perfectly normal. Finnish women claim that if a guy pays for dinner, she "owes" him something—that's some worrying self-esteem right there. She'll try to pay for her half, but resist the urge. Let her pick up the tab after she's slept with you.

DON'T: Talk about the boat you and your buddies bought

Finnish guys get nervous and talk about their favorite thing: Themselves. She doesn't care about your job, your "business", your BMW, your boat, your ex-girlfriend, your iGadget, or your stories from the army. But then again, Finnish guys are getting more Finnish girls than any other nationality—they clearly know what they're doing.

DO: Say nice things

Finnish guys can't express themselves well. Tell her she looks pretty, no, BEAUTIFUL! Compliment her outfit, her perfume. Lie if you have to. Don't say she's got pretty eyes, that's hack. Don't compliment her on her high cheekbones— that sounds creepy.

DON'T: Order a Lonkero

Totally unimpressive. Order wine. Don't worry if you don't understand the wine list, no one does. Don't pretend like you're a wine expert either, you'll get caught. And don't order a cognac after your meal, you're not your dad.

DO: Have manners

In most cultures, fathers teach their sons common courtesies—in Finland these are learned from James Bond films. Don't forget to hold doors open, take her coat, walk behind her, and not get drunk. The jury's still out on whether or not to pull out her chair—at present it's considered kinda lame.

DON'T: Pick her up

You probably don't have a nice car anyway. Just meet her at the restaurant. Dropping her off at home is what you need to be concerned about.

@philschwarzmann – 'Date rape' does not exist
in Finland! Cause no one ever dates.

DO: Use these jokes

This book is comic gold! Feel free to use some of these gems
and make her laugh. Pretend you wrote them yourself, you
have permission.

DON'T: Fiddle with your Nokia N8

Yes, that awesome Nokia N8 with 12MP camera, 16GB of
storage, and Ovi Store full of high quality apps is tempting
to whip out during coffee—resist the urge.

STEP 5: Hitting a homerun

In the year 2000, Bradley University surveyed more than
fourteen thousand people in forty-eight countries about their
number of partners and one-night stands. They were asked
how many people they expected to sleep with over the next
five years and how comfortable they were with the idea of
casual sex. Guess which country, no pun intended, came out
on top?? Finland! No wonder Finns are ranked the happiest
people in the world each year.

So if you arrived to Finland as a single guy, like the Finns
say, you struck the lottery! But if you arrived with a girl
in hand....OOOPS!! You screwed up, cause essentially you
could have had a different girl every night and she'd pay half
the check.

Why are Finns so promiscuous? Is it the long winters,
high alcohol use, strong women's rights, or liberal views? The
French are the world's stereotype for promiscuity. Greeks
consider themselves "lions in the bedroom". And Americans
never can seem to keep their pants on. Yet Finland is still

#1. Why? Religion. Finns visit a church twice in their lives: When they're born and when they die. God doesn't watch you while you're in bed with a stranger, cause God doesn't really exist. Finns are free to express themselves as they wish, without the fear of God's perverted wrath.

American teenagers use baseball metaphors to describe different degrees of sexual intimacy. But this is Finland! We can't use American baseball! So we'll use pesäpallo, Finnish baseball...

1st Base

Smooth move, Steve. After you paid the entire check and used some of this book's killer jokes, you said, "Hey, I got some great wine back at my place." She took the bait. No "third date rule" in Finland!

@philschwarzmann – All the kids who hit the ball and then accidentally ran towards 3rd base aren't retards, they're Finnish.

2nd Base

Merlot is flowing, Barry White is playing—next you pop the question, "Want to take a sauna?" This is the oldest trick in the Finnish playbook. Normally, a question like, "I know we just met, but want to get naked with me?" would get a slap in the face, but the Finnish sauna is NOT sexual! It's perfectly okay for a man and a woman to strip naked together...as long as you're inside a dark and steamy dungeon-like room. Your date can't say "NO" to your request, as this would disgrace Mother Finland and all her traditions.

@philschwarzmann – Women say that "Size doesn't matter".
I wish they wouldn't say that right after I take off my pants.

3rd Base

Easy fella. In Finnish baseball, advancing to 3rd base on your at-bat is considered a "home run", and this situation is no different. Just play it cool. All Finns know there's no sex in the sauna. Not because of tradition, but because of anatomy, you can't get it up in 80°C-degree (176F) heat. In case you're worried about size issues, don't be, that sauna heat will make your package drop to the ground, giving you maximum lengthage. And if you're into that "shaved look" on women, you may be disappointed, as your date has to take saunas with her mother and sister, and fears embarrassment of such a hair style.

@philschwarzmann – Why do guys need to say, "I'm gonna cum"? Is that necessary? And do girls need to yell, "Don't stop! Don't stop!" Have we EVER stopped?

Home Run

After you're out of the sauna, go in for that first kiss, it will be the best first kiss of your life—cause you're both already naked. From there it's easy, the bedroom is just three meters away. Or feel free to stay where you are, Finnish bathrooms are usually massive, half the size of the apartment, so go ahead and explore that space. If you're exhausted from the sauna, turn the washing machine on and let it do the moving for you. Finnish men aren't particularly known for being Don Juans in the bedroom, but neither are Finnish women—so don't worry, rookie.

STEP 6: Move Your Laptop Into Her Place

Oops—shouldn't "engagement" be first, then "marriage", then "moving in"? LOL! No. This is Finland. After a few weeks of spending every waking hour together, you and Mari will realize you're both poor, and paying two rents is just stupid. Finns move out of their parents' house earlier than any other EU country, and it seems they also move in with their boyfriends and girlfriends earlier than any country. One explanation could be that Finland's cost of living is expensive, inspiring couples to move in more quickly—cause moving into a 30sq/m loft is the ideal way to kick off a relationship.

Now you can go ahead and update your Facebook status to "in a relationship", or,"in a relationship with Mari" if you *really* like her.

@philschwarzmann – Some say the true test of love is peeing with the bathroom door open, but I think its taking a shit without turning on the bathroom sink.

STEP 7: Asking The Father For Her Hand In Marriage

In Finland, getting engaged is what two people do on a very drunken night. It's quite normal for Finns to have been engaged several times before settling, all starting at around age fifteen.

No need to surprise her with a diamond, just ask pop the question, then agree on that decision the next day when you've sobered up—that's the romantic way. And no need to ask her father for her hand in marriage, as you're probably thirty-five years old and that would be a bit silly. Occasionally, Mari may propose to Pekka, usually along with an ultimatum, "If you don't marry me, I'm moving on with my life."

The next step is to visit the local Kultajousi jewelry store to pick out engagement bands. You're about to start a serious relationship together, money will be an issue, so you'll need to be thrifty—get something modest, this is no time for romance, cause who cares, she already said 'yes'.

Don't tell everyone you're engaged yet! It's a surprise. You want your friends and family to catch a glimpse of the rings, and then and only then, they'll say, "You're too young to get engaged!"

Next you set a wedding date...five years later. Or maybe never. It doesn't matter at this point—you're already sharing the same fridge. Besides, after several years of cohabitation, the Finnish state automatically makes you common law spouses, receiving almost the same laws as a properly married couple.

STEP 8: The Wedding Day

Congratulations! You made it your wedding day, meaning you have parents or in-laws who can afford to fund it. You survived the common-law trick, fighting, drunken nights with the boys, in-laws, a stag party, a hen party, and a knife fight in Seinäjoki.

The wedding will, of course, take place in Finland, because it's much nicer than your country. It will happen in the summertime, because summers in Finland are heaven. The location will be in the countryside, because it's where people in heaven go to vacation. (Islands off the cost of Finland count as "countryside").

It will be day of traditional Finnish foods, coffee, tango dancing, drinking, awkward speeches, old people, relatives dressed in their "nicest" clothes, cousins you haven't seen in years, your cousins' dates you'll never see again, yellow disposable cameras, cheap wedding gifts, and a female reverend.

Mari will have the option to change her last name. Finns are so full of national pride, they'll want something ending in

–nen. Your surname is something ridiculous like "Zezeran", "Antonov", or "Jahangiri" – so good luck convincing her to take that.

You'd think women who hate their families and fathers so much would be quick to dump off their heritage, but this isn't the case.

If she takes your surname, congrats, you found yourself a keeper— you'll live a long and happy life together, she loves you.

If she goes for the double-barrel hyphenated name, she kinda loves you but is still filled with Finnish pride (like the name "Kerttu" isn't Finnish enough). You'll live a long and happy life together cause she'll bring in a nice salary, as she's wearing the pants in the family.

Your foreign surname brings a lower class to Finland's classless society. Unless she's "famous", if she keeps her own name, she's already got divorce on her mind.

@philschwarzmann – My name is Phil Schwarzmann – but if Timo Soini asks, it's Pili Mustamies. The racists are in power, and my last name is Black man.

STEP 9: Dealing With Problems Around the House

Now that you're living in *Mari's* 30sq/m loft, there could be some clash on rules. You won't have a "den" or "upstairs" to escape to, so it's either spending quality time in the bathroom, or facing Mari head on—or the Finnish way, moping for five days.

Finns don't raise their voices at one another (neighbors may hear), Finns don't throw things (too expensive), Finns don't storm out (Mari will get even more angry)…Finns mope. It's three to five days of talking even less than before. It's a game to see who can hold out the longest. NOTE: Mari will win.

You come from a paternal culture, yet Mari is from a maternal culture – there will be some differences of opinion. Below are a few common problems foreign-Finnish couples have around the house, and how to deal with them...

PROBLEM: Mari has to translate everything for you.

SOLUTION: Remind her that she's the reason you're here. Say, "Fine, let's move to my country. I'd be happy to translate Swahili for you."

PROBLEM: In your country, the woman cooks & cleans.

SOLUTION: You're not in Italy anymore. Start cooking and cleaning very poorly, she'll soon want to do it herself.

PROBLEM: Mari's friends hate switching to English when you're around.

SOLUTION: There's nothing worse than when everyone switches to English just because of you, yet you don't even want to pay attention. Just stop hanging out with Mari's friends—they're boring in both languages.

PROBLEM: You're always the freak at a house party.

SOLUTION: Every party has to have an annoying foreigner. Just wait until everyone gets tipsy, then you'll have plenty of English-speaking friends.

PROBLEM: Mari and you can never see a Finnish movie in the theatres.

SOLUTION: Rent all of Aki Kaurismäki's films and turn the English subtitles on.

PROBLEM: Any task that requires the Finnish language will be Mari's responsibility.

SOLUTION: Normal simple tasks become chores for the language-deprived. Again, remind her how much better life could be back home in Iran.

PROBLEM: You accidently buy olive oil and not vegetable oil. Buying the wrong products from the supermarket makes you feel like a real waste of space.

SOLUTION:. Take her food shopping with you—tell her she should go to S-Market and you'll do Alko.

PROBLEM: Mari will hate spending vacations with your family.

SOLUTION: Summer vacation is finally here! How about a month in Thailand? Or Italy? Or Greece? Or...Wisconsin! Or would Mari rather have your family visit Finland for a month?

PROBLEM: You "forget" to take off your shoes in the house.

SOLUTION: There's no solution to this. She'll divorce you if don't take off your shoes.

PROBLEM: Mari hates that you're "loud" in public.

SOLUTION: And even worse, it's in English! Send text messages to her instead, even if you're holding hands down the street.

PROBLEM: Will you get the baby baptized in the Lutheran Church or Catholic Church?

SOLUTION: Neither, don't partake in silly religious traditions. Your parents will eventually forgive you heathens.

PROBLEM: You can't understand Finnish, so Mari can't discuss Finnish-celebrity gossip with you.

SOLUTION: It's probably best that way.

PROBLEM: Mari will have to hang out with your foreign friends.

SOLUTION: Nothing is more boring than hanging out with a bunch of foreigners who only talk about languages, Finland, and visas. Get some Finnish friends.

STEP 10: Kids?

Finland's aging population needs babies, and it prefers Finnish babies. In fact, fifty percent Finnish is even better as it adds some much-needed diversity in the gene pool. It is your Finnish duty to procreate! And your little blonde haired, blue eyed beauties are guaranteed to come out a-dor-a-ble.

@philschwarzmann – If your Facebook profile photo is a picture of your child…chances are you're ugly.

The Finnish state is on its hands and knees begging you to have a baby— they'll do anything: Near-free pregnancy checkups, low cost child birthing, free box-full-of-baby-stuff that can be turned into a crib, three paid years off work, paid paternity leave, subsidized daycare, free lunches, a tax break, cheap abortions so they don't make the same mistake you did, and free higher education. If you want to get your money's worth in Finland, you need to have a baby.

All Finnish women believe that if they don't have their first child by age thirty, it'll come out retarded. So time is of the essence. She'll graduate around age twenty-eight, after which you'll finally have some free time for travel and hobbies. Then, why not ruin all of that fun with a baby? All of Mari's friends will be having babies so the pressure will be on. Eventually, Mari will convince you to have a child. She'll promise that your life won't change—she'll stay at home while you pursue a career, continue in your salibandy league, play Call of Duty 4 online, and get drunk with your buddies.

She just wants ONE child, after all, but that's of course a trap, cause kids get lonely and need a friend (and the only-children in school were always brats). So you have a second child, but it's another girl, and you want a boy—so ultimately you end up having a third, and fourth...

But look on the bright side—the best part about having a baby is giving it a name – but you can't tell anybody! Finnish baby names are classified information until the Christening. Finns will divulge top-secret information to Russia before they tell you their baby's name.

If you're "James Moore III" and you're expecting" James Moore IV", that tradition will end in Finland. There are no "juniors" here. For bonus points, you might consider having your child's first initial match their last one, so you'd have something in the vein of "Silja Sepponen" or "Marja Mustonen". If you expect your child to travel, you'll want give him/her an international name – cause "Yrjö" sounds even worse abroad.

@philschwarzmann – I've been together with my girlfriend
nearly 10 years and I've finally figured out the secret
of a good sex life...stop masturbating constantly.

STORY My Finnish girlfriend and I first lived in the states together. Before migrating to Finland, I did the American tradition and spent money I didn't have on a diamond ring I couldn't afford, and proposed. Upon entering Finland, my girlfriend reminded me about the Finnish tradition of men wearing an engagement ring. Ten years later, we're still not married, yet I bought a diamond and wear an engagement ring.

6 UNEMPLOYMENT IN FINLAND

WHAT DO I NEED TO GET A JOB?

Finding a job is what will make or break you in Finland. The smart ones come to Finland for a job, the dumb ones come to Finland for a girl, and "being dumb" isn't exactly a sought after skill for potential employers.

When you and Mari first met, all you needed was the air that you breathed. But, before long you needed a Play-Station 3. And Mari needed food. "We could live in a box and be happy!" Remember that? Unfortunately, boxes in Helsinki cost roughly seven-hundred euros a month. Fortunately, Mari is a Finn and won't graduate till she's thirty-nine, so the state will help you pay for your box. Still, it's about time your heartstruck, foreign butt finds a job. Here are some tips...

Unemployment isn't exactly low in Finland, and it seems everyone has multiple Masters degrees. It's no surprise that Finland tops global competitiveness surveys each year. Stiff competition might be healthy for a country overall, but cancerous to individuals who spent their youth smoking pot and chasing Scandinavian girls on AOL Instant Messenger.

Finland also tops global *educational* surveys each year. Every teacher is required to have a Master's degree in teaching, unless you're an English teacher, then the only requirement is that you're an Australian with a drinking problem.

Even McDonald's employees are on the university track. With high student unemployment, they know they're fortunate to have jobs, and delighted to serve you a Big Mac in English even though you could order it in Finnish. That way-too-attractive-for-her-job McDonald's cashier can not only serve you in English, but also in Swedish, Estonian, Russian, French, German, Engrish, and probably Somalian.

Meanwhile you barely speak English, let alone anything else. If you're Scottish, that McDonald's girl speaks even better English than you.

Meanwhile, employees from the untouchables of the Finnish state like the tax office or police station, don't seem to know a word of English. Of course, don't try saying, "Give me my fucking tax card, bitch." She knows what that means.

The hardest obstacle you'll come across in your job search is your lack of Finnish skills. As many foreign job seekers will tell you, even dishwashers need to speak fluent Finnish. Even the guy whose job it is to place tiny stickers on individual tangerines is fluent.

Without Finnish skills you'll be unqualified for about ninety-nine percent of jobs in Finland. That said, the key is to use your native tongue as an advantage. Every decent company needs a native English speaker. Finns make terrible public speakers, shy salespeople, bumbly account directors, and conservative entrepreneurs, and don't know a thing about preparing sushi. So don't think of your language retardation as a handicap, but more of a secret weapon.

My Girlfriend is a Classy Swedish-Speaker! Can Learning Swedish help?

No. This is Finland, not Sweden. It may help you score brownie points with Lotta's parents, or may land you a dishwasher gig in Jakobstad, but Finnish is what you need.

Foreigners who lack proper English skills tend to learn Finnish the fastest and move on to become bus drivers, taxi drivers, tram drivers, or token parliament candidates for political parties who want to prove they're not racist. Foreigners who speak the best Finnish are often the most unemployed, so picking up a computer programming book may be more valuable than that Finnish grammar book.

HOW TO MAKE €€€

Until you master the Finnish language, or more likely, die, here are a few job ideas for the rosey-eyed foreigner:

ENGLISH TEACHER: You got poor grades in English all throughout high school, but in Finland you're good enough to teach it. It's the best job an "Anthropology" major could hope to get—and there's a good chance one of your students will sleep with you.

IT WORKER: The classic job for foreigners, especially if you're Indian. You can come in by ten, leave at three, wear your pajamas, do nothing but surf the internet, and make a respectable salary. Best of all, your mother will tell all her friends that you "work with computers"!

AU-PAIR: For cute, immature girls only. They'll do laundry for some upper-class suburban family to be close to their internet love Mika. They'll learn Swedish rather quickly and learn a lot about Finnish daytime television. And there's a good chance you'll get the husband to sleep with you, then you can get your own place with the blackmail money.

HOOKER: Native Finnish women refuse to become prostitutes, leaving many positions open for Russians, Estonians, and other Eastern Europeans. There's a good chance they'll get a member of Finnish parliament to sleep with them.

AUTHOR: This job is not recommended.

COMEDIAN: Neither is this one.

ENTREPRENEUR: No one will hire you, so hire yourself! You may soon be disappointed with the productivity of your primary employer, as well as strict Finnish regulations and tax codes. Sell anything you want—candles, suspension gel pills, Tupperware, or any other multi-level marketing scam.

STAY AT HOME DAD: Can't get a job but can make babies? Mari was always more into her career anyways—you're just a pretty face. Stay home, change diapers, and develop your "photography career".

CONSTRUCTION WORKER: Don't have a work permit? No problem. Work in the Finnish construction business. Fluency in Estonian required.

@philschwarzmann – Construction crew's been waking me up EVERY morning! So I yelled, "Where's your worker permits!?!?" in Estonian. ...that shut them up.

HOW MUCH SHOULD I LIE ON MY RESUME?

Your prospective employer will receive a Kilpisjärvi-sized stack of resumes for each open position. How do you get yours to stand out? How are Finnish resumes differ from those in your home country? How do you mask the fact that you're a foreigner? Try some of these tips on that next resume update you keep putting off...

Show humility, kinda:

Finns downplay everything they do, never bragging about anything, even on something as important as a resume. But for a good reason—Finns distrust anyone who brags. Bragging is a sure sign someone is lying. Plus, bragging angers the Finnish Lutheran God and brings bad karma onto oneself.

Finns take humility to some ridiculous levels, you need a dictionary to decipher their bashful prose.

"My creative ideas go up and down"
= I'm the CEO of Kone

"My hobbies include feeding the birds"
= I invented Angry Birds

"My company made rubber boots"
= I'm a Senior Vice President at Nokia

"I own a couple magazines"
= I'm the richest person in Finland

So be humble. But no too humble, you need to rise above the rest. Top Finnish managers may show humility, but they're the least humble of their peers as they climb the corporate ladder. Finns expect foreigners to be a bit braggy anyways.

Don't include your previous salary:

It's more than your prospective employer can afford—your high salary will only scare them into thinking you won't stay long for their peanut wages. But most importantly, the practice of including salaries just isn't done in Finland—they can look up your previous years salary online anyway.

Keep it short:

If your resume spills onto a second page, you're giving unnecessary information. Don't be so boastful. And don't mention that you know MS Word, Excel, Outlook and Windows—no one really knows how to use that crap.

Write two resumes, in English:

After eight months of unemployment you'll be ready for that dream dishwashing job. But that "IT Support Desk" position listed on your resume won't help you achieve dishwasher glory, it'll hurt you. Create a second resume that dumbs down your experience and expertise. Cause any job is better than no job!

Should I include a photo?

If you look Finnish even though you're not, then yes.

INTERVIEW WITH A FINN

Arrive on time to your interview. Dress to impress. Fellas, wear a suit. You do own a suit, right? Tucking in your shirt is not enough. Ladies, take off that wedding ring—no employer wants to hire a female who'll be pregnant in a month then out of work for three years. And if your prospective boss is male, he'll think he can eventually sleep with you.

When you meet the employer, do a solid handshake, but none of that macho firm handshake nonsense. Finnish men show off their Far Eastern-similarities by performing a quick bow of the head as they shake for the first time, while Finnish women do a short curtsey as they shake.

Just like the resume, the key to any Finnish interview is to sell yourself while remaining humble. Don't use flakey, grandiose adjectives when describing your personality. Finns hate themselves and you're expected to hate yourself too. Remember that Finns hate "Me Monsters"—eyes towards you, Americans.

Finns are terrible at small talk but have no problem with awkward, silent moments. Of course normal human beings like yourself have a tough time with awkwardness so have some light topics ready. Good topics include: Finland sure is great, Finnish sure is hard, Sweden sure does suck, Saunas sure are hot, Winters sure are long, Finnish girlfriends sure are nice, Traveling sure is necessary, and Bruce Springsteen sure makes great music.

Get ready to be grilled on all the standard foreigner-related questions: Why are you in Finland? No seriously, why? So, how do you like Finland? How's your Finnish? Say something in Finnish. How do you like the weather here? Where do you live? How big is your apartment? Do you own

or rent? How do you like the sauna? Do you like hockey?
Where are you from? I've been there, do you happen to know
this person?

YOUR FIRST DAY ON THE JOB

Congratulations! You got a job! It's not what you had hoped for. It's not what you'd do in your home country. It's not the salary you think you deserve, but it's enough for a used Toyota station wagon and town house in Espoo. And after eight months of unemployment, rug-shaking duties, chronic masturbation and endless "Why are you in Finland?" questions from your mother, you're ready to get out of your apartment and earn a living.

The first day on the job can be nerve-racking, especially in a new country. Will you fit in? Will you make new friends? Can you stomach fish for lunch? Will you miss your daily dose of *The Bold and the Beautiful*?

Your office will be a colorless, cold, and sterile environment. Finnish building codes require lots of windows for sunlight, but eight months of the year your cubicle might as well be in a dark basement. You'd think such a grey country would use more color, but no, steel, wood, and glass are the main materials only—as colorless as the architect's clothes who designed it.

The only sound in your office will be the constant brewing of the coffee machine, as your new colleagues sit silently in front of their PC monitors reading *Helsingin Sanomat* online. The entire office will dart for their mobile phones as the familiar Nokia ringtone fills the air.

No one will introduce themselves. If you're lucky, your new boss will schlep you around the office to meet your new colleagues. They'll be as enthusiastic to meet you as you are to meet them. Again, remain humble—just smile and nod. First impressions are essential—people will quickly hate you if you show any sort of enthusiasm or joy about your new job. You'll forget everyone's name (it was probably "Pekka" or "Mari") and they'll forget yours. If you have an Indian name they'll never remember it, but will remain perplexed as to why you can't remember such ridiculous surnames as "Lemmetyinen" and "Kellokumpu".

For six to eight weeks you should remain as invisible as possible. Finns take a long time to warm up to new people. Any display of extroversion and people will be talking badly behind your back—even a simple "good morning!" could ruin the office culture. So come in to work a bit early, leave a bit late, nod to people at the coffee machine, speak only when spoken to, and be prepared to tell everyone how much you love Finland.

A TYPICAL DAY IN THE OFFICE

Let's take you through a typical day at the Finnish office...

6:30   ALARM! It's pitch black outside, and the sun won't shine for another four hours. Your home is cold—no heating system could combat these winters. You'd love nothing more than to stay underneath these warm covers, but you've got that meeting today. Could this actually be hell? Oh, and you're a bit hungover.

6:40   Snooze button

6:50   Snooze button

7:00   Sure enough, it snowed last night. That means you need an extra twenty minutes to plow your walkway and scrape your car. Your neighbor, Pekka, is already outside plowing—it seems as if he *enjoys* plowing! You loathe him.

7:15   Breakfast: A bowl of porridge. Every Finn knows there's nothing better for you in the morning than porridge! You turn on the TV, catch up with Finnish hockey players in the NHL and last night's handball quarter-finals in Närpes.

7:20   Check *Ilta-Sanomat*. Finnish superstar sensation Johanna Tukiainen is getting married!

7:30   Shower. As sparsely populated as Finland is, the shower is the only place where you get any peace and quiet.

@philschwarzmann – It's never too dark
in the morning if you wake up at noon.

7:45   What to wear? Finns don't wear suits to work. Let's
       open up the dresser to see what clothes your wife
       bought you. How about khaki pants, a "wrinkle-free"
       shirt that looks wrinkled, and a frayed white t-shirt
       to peak above your neckline. You've also got a brown
       belt and brown loafers to match. And a pair of Christ-
       mas socks (no one will see them...yes they will).

7:50   Your hair still looks good from the 30 Euro mall hair-
       cut from last week. The price seemed a bit steep, but
       it was worth every penny to have that young woman's
       breasts rest against your neck for twenty minutes.

8:15   You're late, you spent too much time in the shower.
       You scrape just enough ice from your windshield to
       pull out without hitting any neighborhood kids. Don't
       bother pushing snow off the roof, wind from the high-
       way will handle that for you.

8:16   Your wife is even later, she needs the car, so you take
       the bus. She complains you didn't scrape off enough
       ice. "It's dangerous!"

8:25   The buses are on strike (again). Your next door neigh-
       bor stands at the same bus stop and doesn't even say
       "moi".

8:46   The bus finally comes. Your co-worker is there and
       has a free seat next to him. You escape in the back,
       avoiding eye contact.

8:51   Phew! No traffic. Only the wealthy can afford two cars,
       so most people take public transportation leaving
       the streets wide open for rich people and their Volvo
       XC 90's.

9:17   You're late for work, but it seems you're the first to arrive. Where is everyone? Should you be in some meeting with everyone else? No, it's just that Anna and Hanna are home with sick kids. Sari came back last month after three years on maternity leave, but she's once again pregnant. Pirjo is still out on stress leave. Jussi and Anssi are working from home. Markus is late because of that unexpected February snow. Kirsi gets Mondays off to stay with her kids. Saara is vacationing for a month. Jari is again on a business trip somewhere warm and sunny. Heidi is nowhere to be found, but her last Facebook update came at 3:53am and it said "Fucking wankeredddd!!!"

9:32   You notice that Senja is wearing the same outfit as yesterday. Someone got lucky last night! Or more likely, she's European and has no problem wearing the same clothes two days in a row.

9:39   That psychopath of a boss has been in since 7:30am. His only fulfillment in life is work. His two children will have serious personality disorders later in life. He says, 'Heidi is taking off, she's totally hungover again! LOL!" Everyone has a good laugh.

9:46   Check *Ilta-Lehti*. Finnish star Johanna Tukiainen calls the wedding off.

10:00   First meeting of the day. During the last meeting it was decided to have another meeting before a decision is made. The meeting doesn't kick off until 10:13am cause everyone's late. Half the team is dialing in from home. Someone on the phone clearly has whiney kids. The meeting is constantly interrupted by a dog barking.

10:10   A two minute awkward silence.

10:18   Someone puts themselves on hold, the conference call is ruined by the operator's voice telling you you're on hold. Everyone decides to have another meeting before a decision is made.

10:30   Lunch time! The lunch line already formed at 10:25am Maybe human beings need more than porridge in the morning? Nahh!

10:35   Which meat to choose? Chicken or "game"? Tough choice, but at least you know your sides: Potatoes, chunks of cucumber, dark rye bread, and milk. It was good enough for you in first grade, and it's good enough for you now. For dessert: Some sort of berries drowning in tasteless white goo.

10:48   Talk about the weather with colleagues at the lunch table. And can you believe that Johanna Tukiainen!?!

11:17   Facebook.

12:01   Check *Ilta-Sanomat*. Johanna Tukiainen says wedding is back on!

12:24   Facebook.

13:00   IT guy comes to fix your e-mail. He's the most stoic and depressive person you've ever met.

13:33   Someone makes a racist joke. Someone makes another. Everyone laughs. LOL!

14:05   It's getting dark outside. Feeling tired, depressed. Turn on desk "bright light", now everyone in the office thinks you're crazy. You are.

14:19   Check *Ilta-Lehti*. Johanna Tukiainen wants divorce!

14:30   Another meeting. It's a short one as the outcome had already been finalized last night in the sauna, amongst the men.

14:43   The other office foreigner makes another inappropriate pass at a female colleague. But what are you going to do? He's French! Everyone laughs.

14:44   The office pervert makes another inappropriate pass at a female colleague. HR is notified, but does nothing about it as usual.

15:00   It's someone's pointless birthday! Pulla (cake) time! Which pulla will it be this time? Let me guess. The cinnabon with the cardboard-like outer shell? Totta kai!

15:13   Your boss tells you he needs that project done by "week 43" – you have no idea what "week 43" means.

15:30   Stay clear of the exit door! You may be trampled by a stampede of parents needing to pick up their children from daycare. That report will have to wait until tomorrow!

15:40   Check *Ilta-Sanomat*: Johanna Tukianinen marries ski-jumper Matti Nykanen. Bears child.

16:00   Meeting with your local ad agency. But it's more of a "family reunion" as everyone is related. The business owner is cousins to the account director, and the sales manager is old boyhood friend of the creative director.

16:30   Time to go home, the office is already empty—except Pekka who sits at his desk. It will be for another forty-eight hours until someone realizes he's been dead for days.

16:45   Go directly home. No after work drinks with colleagues. No sports with mates. Go home to your dog. You see your wife everyday, but she says you don't spend enough time together.

STORY: A friendly young Argentinian guy was the janitor in my office building. He too came to Finland for a woman. I felt guilty every week when he cleaned the empty candy wrappers out of my "recycle bin", so I'd strike up a conversation. He told me he was getting his degree in the evenings. I said, "Great! So you can soon give up this cleaning crap?" He replied, "I'm studying to become a professional cleaner." This made me feel even guiltier. So nowadays anytime he comes to empty my candy wrapper-filled recycle bin, I escape to the coffee machine. Only in Finland do you need a college education and legal visa to clean up trash.

7 VITTU!
THE FINNISH LANGUAGE

FINNISH IS THE SECOND HARDEST LANGUAGE IN THE WORLD

For some, learning Finnish will be one of their biggest achievements in life and for many, learning Finnish will be one of their biggest failures. But whether you succeed or fail, learning Finnish will be one of the most challenging tasks you'll ever experience. Yes, you should have met a Swedish girl instead!

Few describe the Finnish language as beautiful, poetic, romantic, or pleasing to the ear. While there's nothing exactly "great" about Finnish, there's nothing "bad" either. There's no gender like Spanish, no pompousness like French, no required hand gestures like Italian, no nasty throat sounds like German, no ear-piercing intonation like Chinese, no silly Cyrillic like Russian, and no fairytale sounds like Estonian.

@philschwarzmann – 93% of Finnish words can be spelled with vowels and the letter 'K'.

Finnish is spoken in monotone, completely devoid of life. Like the hum of an air conditioner, or drone of a car engine, the Finnish language is soothing, if nothing else. You know how the high-pitched babble of Asian girls on a bus breaks your reading concentration? This will never happen with Finnish. You'll concentrate on that book. Finnish babble may even lull you to sleep.

Finnish comes from the Finno-Ugric language family, which includes Hungarian and Estonian amongst others. Estonians can understand Finnish, but Finns can't understand

Estonian—or maybe they can, they just don't care what Estonians have to say.

Except for a few modern words, Finnish looks nothing like English. When you first move to Finland, the Swedish translations will be your guide, as Swedish is a Germanic language like English. With Finnish, you'll just see vowels, umlauts, and the letter K. "Kokko, kokkoo kokkoo koko kokko!" "Koko kokkoko?" "Koko kokko. Kokkookko?" That's a real Finnish conversation! (Albeit a real stupid conversation.)

All Finnish is pronounced the same way—there are no exceptions. There are no sneaky silent letters either. But there are words like Hurskastelevaisehkollaismaisellisuuk-sissaankohankin. Yes. A massive word. And Finnish still doesn't have words for "he" and "she". Finns love their compound words too. You'd think they connect them to save space, right? Wrong! Visit a Finnish movie theatre and you'll see subtitles in both Finnish and Swedish. Nine times out of ten, the Swedish equivalent is shorter. Much shorter.

NOTE: It's not too late to break up with that Finnish girl and find yourself a nice Swedish girl—you'll be fluent in Swedish in a week.

HOW LONG WILL IT TAKE ME TO LEARN FINNISH?

Forever. Or maybe a year. It depends. Some say "You'll learn Finnish when hell freezes over." During your first winter here, you'll realize that has already happened and your Finnish still begins with "moi" and ends with "moi moi".

English is supposedly like a triangle. You start at the bottom where the base is wide and you quickly learn a lot, but as you improve the triangle gets smaller and you learn less. Like Superman's emblem, Finnish is like an upside triangle. At the bottom you learn very little, and by the time you get to the top you've already given up. You're no Superman.

But if you decide to climb that triangle-shaped ladder, here are some tips to help you learn Finnish...

DON'T BE AMERICAN/ENGLISH/CANADIAN/AUSTRALIAN: Or any other native-English speaker. You were never properly taught a second language in school.

DON'T RELY ON OSMOSIS: Think you can just move to Finland, look at some billboards, and eventually pick up the language? Think again! Learning Finnish takes dedication, perseverance, and a hundred and twenty euros a semester for classes.

TAKE CLASSES: In class, you'll meet other pathetic individuals like yourself who left their country for a caliber of woman they couldn't get in their hometown. But if you're single, you're in luck as ALL Finnish teachers are female—desperate, broke, females who LOVE foreign men. Why else would they teach Finnish to foreigners? They get men right off the boat, they're like chefs going to the market at 5AM for the freshest fish.

HIRE A TUTOR: Your chances of sleeping with her are almost guaranteed. Unfortunately, they're rarely that cute.

DON'T BE AFRAID OF MISTAKES: You finally learned English, now you're giving it up and starting from scratch. Not only do car mechanics know more about cars than you, they know more about language. Yes, it's frustrating. Suck up that pride and speak broken Finnish.

SPEAK FINNISH WITH KIDS: Kids understand the difficulties of learning another language, cause they're struggling with it too. They're even better than hiring a tutor.

TRADE OFF DAYS AT HOME: Mari will be your biggest advocate. She wants you to learn Finnish so she can keep you here forever. For one full day, speak English. Then the next day, speak Finnish. On Finnish days you'll think you're turning Finnish as you have little to say. Then on your English days you and Mari will have so much catching up to do!

WWW.FINNISHSCHOOL.COM: A great way to learn the Finnish vocabulary. Think of it as virtual flash cards.

GET A JOB THAT REQUIRES FINNISH: No foreigner learns Finnish faster when they're just thrown in to the pit and forced to use Finnish. It's nightmarish the first six months, but you'll learn—or be unemployed.

@philschwarzmann – I speak with a bit of an accent,
or as I like to call it, speaking perfectly normal.

TODDLERS SPEAK FINNISH, WHY CAN'T YOU?

Finns love to ask foreigners, "So how's your Finnish??" They say this with a smirk on their face as they know their language is hard. After a few months in the country, you can reply, "Moi!" and everyone will laugh. After a year in the country, you can reply, "Hyvin menee!" and everyone will be so proud. After about eight years and a daily reminder about how bad your Finnish is, you can reply honestly: "It's not going well. I hate Finnish. It's completely useless. It sounds worse than fingernails across a chalkboard. If AIDS had a sound, it would sound like Finnish. Stephen Hawking has a sexier accent. It's not that it's difficult, nor am I lazy – it's just that I don't want to learn it." Everyone knows that Finns appreciate honesty. That response will test it.

Even your fellow foreigners will bust your chops for not speaking Finnish. They'll rave about their great Finnish, but when you actually hear it, rest assured they just use the same ten words over and over again, but with the confidence of a native speaker. It's embarrassing. Those who boast about their Finnish skills speak it the most poorly.

If you take a Finnish class subsidized by the state, the class will most likely be "Finnish in Finnish", which means they only use Finnish. This would be fine, but you don't speak Finnish, that's why you're in the class. They want to submerse you into the Finnish language, but you already live in Finland. It's like teaching people to swim by throwing them in.

Your Finnish teacher will first teach you 'written' Finnish. Once you learn that, she'll remind you that no one actually speaks like that. If you speak like that, everyone will think you're a foreigner, or President Halonen doing her Christmas address. You need to learn 'spoken' Finnish! Finnish prose is so long, they've shorted it for speech. Why don't Finns say "Minä rakastan sinua" (I love you) to each other? Obviously it's got too many syllables.

The Finnish public will not help you either. As soon as you attempt Finnish, they'll recognize your accent and switch to English—they think they're doing you a favor. People either speak Finnish or they don't, Finns aren't accustomed to any foreigners who kinda-sorta know the language. They don't know how to dumb down their vocabulary and slow down their speech. If you don't understand them, they'll just repeat the exact same thing, but louder, and in some weird Savo dialect while they roll their R's for seven seconds.

Finns will tell you about the many "crazy" dialects that exist in little Finland. "Those people who live in that city an hour away speak like THIS, while we speak like THIS!" Just smile and nod. "Yes yes, it's soooo different!"

HOW-TO SPEAK FINNISH LIKE A FINN

Once you've mastered the language, you won't want people to know you're a foreigner. Follow these easy steps to speak Finnish just like a Finn...

SPEAK QUIETLY: Only drunk people, Swedish speakers, and Americans speak loudly. Speaking loudly in public will bring embarrassment to yourself. And worst of all, Finns are listening. Finns' favorite pastime is to listen closely to strangers' conversations, then share those conversations on Internet forums hours later.

DON'T USE YOUR HANDS: This is Northern, not Southern, Europe—keep your hands to your sides. Any sort of hand gesture will show that you're lying and cannot be trusted. Besides even if you wanted to flail your arms, you can't, they're too stiff from the cold weather.

DON'T USE INTONATION: Emotionless and cold as a Finnish winter, your voice should remain monotone like an Isaac Asimov-inspired robot. Exception: When answering the phone, go overboard with your own name: "Tommmmm-mmmmmmmmmi Kuuppelomäki terve!!"

MEN, SPEAK SLOWLY: If the pace of your speech is a like a cassette player on low batteries, you're speaking too fast. After a question is posed to you, take a pause. Then another pause. Make no facial movements whatsoever. When those first words do leave your lips, they shouldn't be real words—use something "siis", "niin", "no", or "jooooo".

WOMEN, SPEAK QUICKLY: If the pace of your speech is like a 33rpm record being played at 45rpm – you're speaking too slowly. When you do speak, don't pause for breaths. Instead, wait until you're about to pass out from lack of oxygen, then gasp violently for air while saying "joo!", then get back to yapping.

LOOK AT FEET: Like the classic joke says, "How do you tell if a Finn is an extrovert? He looks at your shoes, not his own!"

NEVER GIVE A FINITE ANSWER: Finns are constantly unsure of themselves as answering a question directly may come back to haunt them. Whenever someone asks you a YES or NO question, confidently reply, "Yes AND no..."

SAY WHAT YOU MEAN: If you say, "Let's meet for lunch sometime!", you're going to meet for lunch sometime. In other languages, especially American English, saying "Let's meet for lunchtime sometime!" means, "Bye!"

USE AS FEW WORDS AS POSSIBLE: It's cold out, there's no time to jibber-jabber. When approaching a dog park, don't say, "Hi! May I ask, is your dog a male or female? My dog has some difficulties with older males." Just yell, "BOY OR GIRL!!!" Me Tarzan!

EVERY OTHER WORD SHOULD BE "NIINKO": Just do it.

STORY: After being unemployed my first few months in Finland and running out of savings, I received a bill from the Finnish tax office. I was being charge several hundred euros for the "non-Finnish" letters in my surname. The letters 'c', 'w', and 'z' are challenging for Finnish children to pronounce, and the money was to help young Finns with speech impediments. I was furious! This is so like the "socialist" tax office! I went to the Internet to air my grievances. Before I could login, my girlfriend asked, "What's today's date?" I said, "April 1st!! Why!? …ohhhhhh, damn it!" The best April Fool's prank ever.

8　A FINN OUT OF WATER

FINNS ON HOLIDAY

Remember it's "holiday", not "vacation". A vacation is what an American takes. Holiday is what a Finn takes. What's the difference? Finnish holidays are at least five weeks per year. An American vacation lasts just two. Even if Americans *claim* they get three or more weeks vacation, everyone knows they get just two. Unless you're the U.S. president, then you get about seventeen weeks.

Finnish law dictates that each individual receive at least five weeks holiday. Those five weeks are traditionally split between four summer weeks and one winter "ski week". Those four summer weeks are usually taken in succession during the month of July. Taking summer holiday outside of July can be forbidden at some jobs—you'll often hear Finns say, "Voi voi! I'm forced to take four weeks in a row during July!" Yes yes, life is sometimes so tough.

@philschwarzmann – This holiday I'm going to either
1) Get in shape or 2) Get a tan – Both achieve the same goal.

Technically Finns get thirty days of holiday per year, but five of those days must be Saturdays. "But no one works on Saturdays! So it's technically five weeks holiday, right?" you ask. "No! You can't forget Saturdays." The whole thing makes no sense. Finns claim they understand this concept, but they don't. It's the biggest riddle you'll find in Finland.

If you return from holiday, each Finn receives two weeks bonus salary. Why "*if* you return"? In yesteryears, Finns would binge drink throughout their holiday, so the state had to encourage alcoholics to return to work. Finland, you're an enabler!

Finns spend more of their disposable income on holidays than any other European country. Isolated so far in the north, Finns must hop on a plane if they wish to visit any place warm and/or interesting (Turku is not interesting). They mock countries that receive such little holiday time, then wonder why their salaries aren't nearly as high.

Five weeks of expensive Helsinki departures are more than the average person can afford. So much of your "holiday" is spent visiting relatives, "relaxing at home", cleaning your summer cabin, chopping firewood for your summer cabin, being bored at your summer cabin, and drinking in your bathtub. You know, stuff that'll make you wish you were back in the office surfing the Internet.

HOW TO IDENTIFY A FINN ON HOLIDAY

Look for the couple drinking beer. In Helsinki-Vantaa airport. At 6am. They'll have a look on their face that looks like they're waiting for the plane to Auschwitz.

Holiday is the one day a year you're allowed to start drinking before 10am without fear of embarrassing your fellow countrymen. By the time you reach your economy class seat, you'll be sauced and ready for vacation, and ready to harass the flight attendant as well as your wife. Tax free booze, woo-hoo!

That couple that you mistakenly thought were deaf were just Finnish. Finns barely whisper, let alone speak. If they do speak, they're probably ridiculing the trashy Ed Hardy-wearing Russian family at the next table. "Kulta, isn't it gross how that Russian girl is wearing a black thong with white pants?" "Errr...yes, rakas."

Finns don't want to bring attention to themselves, especially from other Finns. There's nothing worse for a Finn abroad than seeing another Finn. Hearing the Finnish language abroad brings a cringe down the spine. At any moment, your fellow Finn could do something to embarrass themselves, their family, country, and therefore...you. After all, you purchased this expensive vacation to escape from Finns! NOTE: Swedes have class and NEVER do anything embarrassing abroad.

Like vampires, Finns avoid the sun as their skin quickly bakes from bright white to Lappish-midnight-sun-pink in minutes. You'll know it's a Finn cause they'll be the only ones wearing pants in +40°C heat. Ever seen a pair of pale Finnish legs up close? Shudder.

Finns don't own clothes for +25°C weather and above. They're tough to find in Finland. So look for the Finn wearing a cheap Hawaiian shirt from that Canary Island trip in the Eighties, a neon colored fanny pack, leather pouch for a Nokia 9210i Communicator, Speedo, baseball cap with the name of the country they're currently visiting, khaki pants (no belt), and of course the dreaded sandals-with-socks.

Don't expect to find a Finn at the local restaurant experimenting with "foreign" cuisine. All Finns know that food produced outside of Finland, especially food produced outside of Europe, is dangerous and will give you food poisoning. Just like foreign people, foreign food should not be trusted. So look for Finns piling up their plates with meat and potatoes as normal. Also, foreign coffee is NEVER as good as the Finnish brands, so pack your own along with a few bags of Jenki gum and rye bread.

Finally, look for a confused family standing in a line wondering why they're there. When Finns see a line, and they feel they need to stand in that line.

WHERE TO TRAVEL ON HOLIDAY

In need of an escape from Finland? You're in luck! There are a million places to visit! A "million" being, anywhere Finland's three major travel agencies will take you. Here are your options...

Tallinn, Estonia

Finally! A country Finland can look down upon. While Norway looks down on Sweden, Sweden looks down on Finland, and Finland finally looks down on Estonia. (And Estonia looks down on Latvia.) Humble Finland bashfully gazes at its *own* shoes when addressing countries of the world but with their southerly neighbors, Finland stares at Estonia's shoes.

If Finland's borders are in the shape of a maiden, then Estonia clearly is the rug underneath. Situated just two ferry ride hours away from Helsinki is Estonia's capital city, Tallinn. Its historic old town will make you feel like you're in Europe!

Known as the "Disney*world* of Finland" this inexpensive weekend getaway is perfect for those in search of cheap booze, hookers, blindness, a bar dedicated to Depeche Mode, knit mittens, and all around debauchery. Finns take the 80km booze cruise to Tallinn, run amok, and while in their drunken stupor, get robbed, cheated, and beaten up. Then they retreat home calling Estonia, "dangerous and unsafe!"

@philschwarzmann – Estonians think Finns are alcoholics, but they're alcoholics too—the only difference is, Finns have money to get drunk abroad.

Stockholm, Sweden

Depart on a cruise ship in the evening and arrive in Sweden's capital by morning. Stockholm is perfect and far superior to Helsinki in every way. It has everything: an old town, royalty, diversity, a proper subway, beautiful architecture, great shopping, well-dressed beautiful non-drunk super-people, ABBA, naked blondes in pigtails directing traffic, and Volvo.

But no Finn on a cruise to Stockholm cares about any of that! Cruising to Stockholm is all about the cruise itself. The booze cruise. It's a night of partying, followed by a day of hangover, followed by a night of partying, followed by a day of apologizing, followed by a pregnancy test, followed by a visit to the clinic, followed by lunch. More girls have lost their virginity on the Stockholm boat than in Allah's suicide bomber heaven.

Canary Islands, Spain

Known as the "Disney*land* of Finland", this has been the most popular Finnish tourist destination since Finns could afford air travel. Due to the density of Finns there year round, the Canary Islands could technically be an autonomous territory of the Finnish state.

Here you'll find restaurants with Finnish menus, nightclubs owned by Finns, Finnish karaoke bars, Finnish vodka in supermarkets, and Finns who are drunk 24/7. It's one of the most affordable tourist destinations with packages starting around five hundred euros, so you have more money to spend on alcohol.

Thailand

What are the chances of a tsunami hitting the same country twice in a decade? Very little, let's hope. Thailand is still one of the most popular tourist destinations as the weather is warm and sunny year round.

Want to impress your Finnish friends? Whenever they say "Thaimaa*seen*" (which means, "to Thailand"), correct them and say "Thaimaa*han*"—Finns always get this wrong.

Mariehamn, Åland Islands, Finland?

Situated between Finland and Sweden, but much closer Sweden, the Swedish-speaking Åland Islands are a semi-autonomous region of Finland. With just twenty-eight thousand inhabitants, rivaling the size of Lichtenstein or an East Philadelphia housing project, the Åland Islands have an unnecessarily large parliament that spends their days legalizing snus and trying to remove the "semi-" from "semi-autonomous".

Tourists often visit Åland by taking their their bicycles on a cruise to Stockholm. They depart at about 4am when the ship floats by Åland's capital "city", Mariehamn. It's their first and last time in Åland, as on their return home they vow to "never to be such a cheap bastard and take such a lame vacation ever again! Sorry, kids."

Silja Line vs. Viking Line

Finns participate in a continuous debate as to which is the better cruise liner—it's like choosing between death by fire or death by firing squad. Both are cheap, both will get you tax free booze, and both will get you laid if you don't pass out before midnight.

Americans and Brits beware: Don't tell Finns about the cruising you're accustomed to. Finns have never been on a proper cruise (yet they see the giant foreign ships parked in Helsinki's harbor each summer day) and will assume you spend two weeks on something too similar to Viking Line (which, as everyone knows, is even worse than Silja Line).

Winter Destinations

Foreigners may get jealous of Finland's long holidays but Finns withstand six maddening months of winter, so come February, a warm week abroad is desperately needed and deserved....unless you're a masochist who prefers skiing.

Each February/March the entire country takes a "ski week". The schools shut down, parents take off work, dogs go to the in-laws, and Finland's middle and upper classes go on holiday. But not all at once. They can't have the entire country gandala-ing up to Lapland at one time (AVALANCHES!). So the country takes turns. The best region goes first: Southern Finland. Then the second best: Central Finland. Then the reindeer herders and forest people take a week off from being unemployed and go last: Northern Finland.

Finns must do their patriotic duty to patronize a Finnish ski resort. It's sacrilegious to ski in Sweden or the Alps. "Resorts" like Ylläs, Ruka, and Levi need Finnish euros to survive, as British tourists are just a couple years away from realizing what a huge scam Santa's Village is.

Why don't flashy Europeans ski in Finland? Simply put: Finland is completely flat. It's the #1 misconception foreigners have about Finland. Finland needs implants. But Shhhhh....don't tell anyone! It's Finland's best kept secret. If you migrate to Finland, get ready to answer such questions from your family like "So I guess you do a lot of downhill skiing?" and get ready to lie. As denying the holocaust in Germany, don't be surprised if Finnish politicians makes it a criminal offense to deny tall Finnish mountains—they need those guillable Finnish tourists to keep coming to Lapland! Monty Python almost let the moose out of the bag with their 1971 song, "Finland". "Finland, Finland, Finland, the country where I quite want to be. With mountains so *lofty*, and treetops so tall."

Here's Finland's second best kept secret: No one actually *likes* skiing. Who wants to do the exact same thing over and over again all week long? But when there's snow six months of the year, and you're surrounded by such huge mountains (wink wink), you need to have something to do to pass the long, dark depressing days of winter. It's like prison inmates and gang rape: You better learn to enjoy it, cause there's not much else to do.

HOW TO AVOID YOUR FAMILY'S SUMMER CABIN

Every proper Finn longs to spend the rest of their days at a summer cabin—or "mökki" in Finnish. Jobs, school, car payments, and Finnish Idol are all just obstacles in the way of quality time at the cabin. Like temples sprinkled around the country, the cabin is the closest Finns get to any sort of religion.

The Finnish summer cabin is a place of beauty, tranquility, family, yesteryear, simplicity, self-reflection, and tattered playing cards. Every child has fond memories of summers at the cabin, every parent has fond memories of time with their children at the cabin, every teenager has fuzzy memories of parties at the cabin, every couple has warm memories of romantic escapades at the cabin, and every grandparent has proud memories of actually building that cabin.

With 144,000 cabins in Finland, it often feels as if every family has their very own lake. Nestled deep in the forest, or if you're Swedish-speaking, along the coast or archipelago, the family cabin is most likely built by the man of the house, his brothers, and a neighbor. If the cabin was screwed up in any way, it was built with the help of some Russian guys.

A visit to the Finnish summer cabin is like a trip back in time. There's no running water so you'll need to fetch it up from the lake. There's no toilet, so you'll enjoy an outhouse. There may not be any electricity so you'll read. Don't worry if you forgot a book, they'll be plenty of old newspapers and magazines from the Nineties laying around for your nostalgic pleasure. "Tanja Karpela divorces!" Oh my!

A day at the cabin is a busy one—there are many chores to do. If fetching your own water isn't enough, the cabin is constantly in need of a cleaning and the garden needs tending. As one meal finishes it's time to prepare the next, the yard needs mowing, the kids are bored to tears, something always needs fixing, and there's literally an eternal amount of wood chopping to be done. Every true Finnish man knows there's never, ever enough firewood.

To sum it up: Life at the Finnish cabin is a huge nightmare. You'd rather be at work. At least at the office you won't have to pour mulch on your own feces (unless you work at KONE). And your annoying kids aren't around.

If the cabin's hard labor doesn't bite you in the ass, the mosquitos will. With only three months of borderline decent weather, God reminds Finns how much he hates them by unleashing the mosquitos. While most vacationers return home with a suntan in check, Finnish cabiners plod back to civilization wearing mosquito bites as stripes. There's no way to prevent them—smoke from the green-mosquito-smoke-coils only deter humans, mosquitos appear to have acquired a taste for bug spray, and every time a Finn quits the Lutheran Church, the mosquitos grow stronger.

The only thing worse than mosquitos at your cabin is extended family! These leeches arrive unexpectedly, never bringing anything of their own. They raid your food, drink your beer, and don't participate in any chores. That alcoholic father of yours didn't leave your kids with any money, but did leave a dilapidated cabin for the four of you to fight over. You can't abandon it, as that will anger the family. You can't sell it as it's been in the family for years, and it's worth nothing. And you're not about to give it to your sister Sari cause she gets everything! So the kids share the cabin and complain that Sari stays there all the time yet does the least work on it. Sari's husband, your brother-in-law, is a jerk. The entire family fights.

Nothing is more of a love-hate relationship for Finns.

STORY: I was talking to this girl in the states, I told her I live in Finland and she said, "Oh I've been there!" I said, "Cool! How'd you like it?" She said, "Well, Finland kinda sucked. It was cold, dark, and rainy...and the plane was late." I said, "Uhhh, where exactly in Finland did you visit?" "The airport...I had a layover on my way home from Germany."

9 A ONE-WAY TICKET HOME

Heading back so soon? Were the apartments too small? Was the nightlife too dull? Did the dessert have too many bananas in it? Was your company finally sold to the Americans? Oh, she broke up with you via text message? You never learned the language, did you? Or maybe it was the weather? Yeah, it was the weather.

On your way home, you'll kiss goodbye to all the bad things Finland brought. But within days you'll long for all those great things—the liberal attitudes, the homogeneity, the closeness to nature, the simple life, the peace and quiet, and, of course, the cute Finnish girls.

The years you spent in Finland will be some of the best of your life. You learned another language, another culture. Whatever you experienced in Finland will be with you forever. If only you could combine Finnish culture with the culture from your home country. But alas, you can't.

There's no place like Finland.

WAS MANNERHEIM GAY?

Yes.

STORY: During my most recent visit to my family in Baltimore, there was a little confusion at customs. My girlfriend and I stood in separate lines, one for citizens, and the other for possible terrorists. The customs officer asked who I was traveling with. "I'm with my girlfriend, she's in the other line, she's Finnish." The customs officer replied, "What's 'Finnish'?" I very politely explained, "Finnish is someone who is from Finland." She said, "Oh, I wouldn't know that, I'm not very 'worldly'". Not very worldly!?! You're a U.S. customs officer! You meet more foreigners in one hour than I'll meet in my entire life! You're quite possibly the most 'worldly' person I've ever met!

ACKNOWLEDGEMENTS

Massive thanks to all friends, family, and colleagues who've supported my comedy and writing endeavors. Especially to Gummerus and my editor Ilpo Jäppinen for believing in this book. Heidi Lemmetyinen for kickstarting me into the publishing world. Ali Jahangiri, Louis Zezeran, Lei Sorvisto, and James Beechinor-Collins for their positive support. Mom, Mel, and Tom for lending me out to Finland. Nokia for always supporting the creative extracurricular ambitions of its employees. And to anyone who's ever laughed at one of my jokes.

Special thanks to Carl Gustaf Emil Mannerheim for his exclusive posthumous interview.